I0796004

THE CATECHIST'S FORMATION WORKBOOK

The CATECHIST'S FORMATION WORKBOOK

10 SESSIONS ON DEVELOPING AND THRIVING AS A CATECHIST

TWENTY-THIRD PUBLICATIONS
twentythirdpublications.com

This workbook is based on and adapted from *Into the Fields* ©2006 by Twenty-Third Publications.
(Spiritual Exercises in *Into the Fields* ©2006 Dan Schutte.)

Cover photo: ©iStockphoto.com /gabrieleckert

TWENTY-THIRD PUBLICATIONS
1 Montauk Avenue, Suite 200, New London, CT 06320
(860) 437-3012 » (800) 321-0411 » www.twentythirdpublications.com

ISBN: 978-1-62785-251-7
Printed in the U.S.A.

A division of Bayard, Inc.

Contents

Introduction

So, you are starting a new year of catechesis! Many experiences await you to help both you and your learners grow as disciples of Christ. Whether you are a brand new catechist or teacher or have already taught for a few years, we hope you will learn from and enjoy the material in *The Catechist's Formation Workbook.*

The Catechist's Formation Workbook is rooted in Scripture, liturgy, and the *Catechism of the Catholic Church* and is based on both the *General Directory for Catechesis* (GDC) and the *National Directory for Catechesis* (NDC).

Each of the ten sessions in this volume begins with prayerful reflection. These brief reflections invite you to begin your time of study by considering your own experience of God's love. A reflection question and space for you to record your thoughts lead to a time of prayer.

Tools for Teaching is the formal teaching section, providing the connecting link between spiritual growth, content of the faith, and instructional strategies needed to do excellent catechesis.

Step one sets the tone with an introductory story or exercise.

Step two helps you reflect on the significance of the topic for catechesis.

The three sections of material that follow guide you in implementing the objectives, using theory, practical commentary, and examples, plus strategies for different age levels. Also included are questions for personal use and group discussion to help you integrate what you have learned.

You may be invited to attend a group session in which you will discuss the material and share with other catechists. These gatherings will help you grow both spiritually and professionally. Instructions are provided throughout on how to make the most of the various elements, whether you are studying alone or with a group. Read the appropriate section in *Tools for Teaching* and reflect on the questions as you study or before each large group session. Keep this volume close by while you are teaching, as well as while you are studying. It is not meant to sit on your shelf!

Remember: you are a very important figure for your learners. You are a living witness of the faith you seek to share with them. Your example speaks volumes. You never know when, through you, the Spirit will touch the hearts of your learners. God's grace works in mysterious ways. Even when you think a lesson may seem to be a complete failure, your kindness, your enthusiasm, your willingness to speak the truth, any or all of these, may make an impression on one or more of those you teach.

So we hope you will make the most of this book and all it contains. It has been prepared with much care, research, and prayer. May your basic catechetical skills and attitudes continue to grow by leaps and bounds!

SESSION

1

Preparing yourself *and* your learning space

The goal of this session is to prayerfully and effectively prepare for your learning session.

YOUR OBJECTIVES ARE:

- to continue your spiritual formation through prayerful reflection on the love of God
- to learn ways to prepare carefully and prayerfully before each session
- to learn how to promote an atmosphere in which the learners feel welcome
- to learn how to organize the teaching space

SKILL: Prepare a welcoming, organized space for learners

BEGINNING THIS SESSION

Before you begin to develop your skill in preparing a learning space, take a few moments for reflection and prayer.

Seeing ourselves and others with God's eyes

God is in love with us. And so, like a good lover, God courts us and woos us with signs and symbols of love. When we don't get it, God tries again and again, all the while hoping that we will finally take notice. And God won't give up until we finally get the message. When we finally allow God to love us, the power of that love is transforming.

Many of us struggle all our lives to believe that we are lovable and have unique value. Sometimes we've convinced ourselves in the depth of our soul that we are not lovable, that our life doesn't really make a difference. If you struggle with such feelings, it is important to ask God to open your heart to love.

God sees us just as we are and yet loves us beyond words. God's love does not depend on our holiness or perfection. Even beyond that, there is nothing we can do to earn God's love. It is simply a freely given, gracious gift.

What if we could see ourselves and others as God sees us? Are we not the apple of his eye? What possibly could keep God from loving us? The truly amazing thing is that there is nothing at all, not even sin, that can keep God from loving us.

Take a moment to reflect

Ask yourself: How has the hand of God been present in my life?

The time of prayer
As you move from reflection to study, take a moment to pray for yourself, your learners, and your time together in catechesis.

Dear God, Lord of my life, I sit in awe
before the gaze of your love.
It is sometimes difficult to let
you love me in this way.
I'm not used to its power and warmth.
But I want to let your love transform me so
that I can become a better disciple,
a better teacher and bearer of your Word.
Set me ablaze with the fire of that love.

From personal reflection to sharing faith
As a catechist, you have the opportunity to share the transforming love of God with your learners. In this session, you will develop skill in preparing your learning space in order to create an environment in which your learners may open their minds and hearts to this incredible love of God for us.

TOOLS FOR TEACHING

> Catechists are to identify and create "suitable conditions necessary for the Christian message to be sought and accepted." **NDC 54B.8**

Setting the tone
"Be faithful, then, in following the example of Jesus; be strong and firm in faith, and love the community as you love one another. Remain united in the truth and be as gentle as the Lord in dealing with one another, looking down on no one. If you can do good, do not hesitate, for charity frees us from death."[1]

The importance of this session

- How do you make your learning space a sacred space? Welcoming? Effective?
- Prepare yourself with prayer and become familiar with the content of the material you intend to share.
- Remember an experience of welcome in the parish community that you enjoyed. Consider why it was a welcoming experience, and incorporate that into your own efforts at welcoming your learners.
- Prepare your teaching space in a way that emphasizes your theme for that lesson.

Step one: *prepare yourself*
Love is the motivating force for your own preparation. In a sense you have made a covenant as God did with his prophets and his people: to proclaim God's word. In order to teach your learners about God, you will want to emulate God's teaching style. You can do this by reflecting on the word of God, by reflecting on the experience of gathering in the Sunday assembly, by praying for your

1 *Share the Light*, St. Polycarp, Letter to the Philippians.

learners, and by knowing the content of the material well.

STRATEGIES FOR PREPARING YOURSELF

Refer to your catechist's or teacher's manual for specific suggestions for your lesson. Then read through these strategies.

- Preparing yourself allows you to be clear about your focus—that is, the learners—to pace yourself, and to visualize yourself teaching. After all, your witness and enthusiasm are important factors in teaching the lesson.

- Be prepared for the unexpected. Prepare alternate activities in case those you planned don't work out; have a "Plan B" in case a guest speaker doesn't show up, or your media equipment doesn't function properly, or for other unexpected circumstances.

- In the Sunday assembly, you gather with your faith community to celebrate God's love and your faith response. The welcome and unity of the assembly can be a model for welcoming your learners.

- Pray for yourself and your learners. You may want to keep a list of their names on hand so you can think of and pray for their needs as individuals, not just as a group.

Step two: *prepare your learning space*

Having a well-prepared learning space can pique the interest of the learners and invite them to participate in the sessions. Preparing or adding something related to the lesson to the meeting space or classroom will appeal to the imagination of your learners. Refer to your textbook manual for ideas. Have a focus object (something related to the lesson that will capture their attention), name tags they can create or that are already prepared, or some age-appropriate activity that will engage early arrivals. Keep in mind their age level—whether children, youth, high school students, or adults—in preparing your teaching space, and incorporate in some way a visible element of the liturgy.

Keep in mind the interests and needs of your learners in preparing the teaching space.

Younger children like objects they can touch, smell, and so forth. Older learners, including adults, are stimulated by puzzles and objects that challenge them to think.

Step three: *make learners feel welcome*
Hospitality and welcome go far beyond a simple greeting. In addition to the detail we give to preparing the learning space and creating a good learning environment, we also want to engage learners by name and to help them participate in creating a warm learning environment for their fellow learners. In the first gatherings, name tags are very important, not only to help people feel a sense of belonging but also to allow them the freedom of engaging with others whom they may not know too well. As the entire group begins to address each other by name, the importance of each learner is implicitly affirmed, as well as their presence and their contribution to the group as a body. Appropriate sharing of our life experiences fosters a culture of mutual trust and affirmation, which is especially vital to the adult learning experience.

STRATEGIES FOR CREATING A WELCOMING ATMOSPHERE

- Every learner, no matter what age, has different abilities and his or her own way of learning. Be alert to the need to affirm and honor cultural and individual diversity, and encourage the learners in expressions of their uniqueness. Point out that each of us brings different gifts to the church, and so we add to God's family. We can all learn from one another. We each bring unique gifts to the learning process through our different styles and ways of learning.

- Create a learner-centered environment in which learners understand that their needs have priority over the planned session. Let them know that you give your time freely because you care about them and their growth as followers of Jesus. Show empathy. Try to see the world through their eyes. No matter what age you teach, talk to your learners at their level. Show respect for their thoughts and recognize their insights. Help them express themselves if necessary. Never "put down" a learner or ridicule him or her.

- Draw out the learners who tend to

Having a well-prepared learning space can pique the interest of the learners and invite them to participate in the sessions.

be silent, but also challenge those who express themselves more freely. Show respect to both introverts and extroverts. Expect the best from all the learners, whatever their age. Stretch their minds and hearts through activities, questions, liturgical experiences, outreach programs, and so on. Keep communication open between you and each learner.

- Above all, share your joy in accompanying them on their faith journey. Present loving images of God. Show through your own example what the learner's relationship with God can be, especially as a part of your parish family.

Step four: *make your teaching space a welcoming, sacred space*

Catechists often teach in many different surroundings: a church, a meeting hall, a classroom, a living room, a church basement. The physical setup of your teaching space is important for "planting the seed" of God's word, for hearing God's word, but any environment can become a welcoming and sacred space if you keep the following elements in mind.

Through these activities, help your learners enter into the mystery of Jesus and celebrate his presence among us:

- Create a "prayer space" and let it be the central focus of your learning environment. The prayer space can be as simple as a corner with a few flowers and a Bible; a table covered with a cloth or a banner; a crucifix or other image according to the season, such as a Bible, a candle (be careful about fire codes), and so on. The prayer station will help make it clear that Jesus is the center of your lessons, of your whole program.

- Plan your seating arrangement. If at all possible, arrange the seats in a circle, semicircle, clusters, or some formation that allows you and the learners to interact more easily. (If you share the use of the room with another class, be sure to return the chairs to their proper places when you are done.) The seating arrangement also assists in managing behavior with younger learners and youth.

You can separate talkative learners, place those who are "attention seekers" farther in back, and place learners who need more assistance closer to you.

- Make the room more attractive and functional by using pillows, small rugs, and plants. Have an activity center where learners can do alternate activities if they finish the group work early or where learners can process the lesson on their own.

- If you are a catechist and share your teaching space with others, bring objects and materials with you that relate to the lesson. Keep the materials together in a box, bag, or something else that is easily portable. Teachers may already have areas to keep their materials organized and at hand.

- You may often be able to obtain resources from local merchants: for example, large boxes from appliance stores, rug samples from carpet stores, paint and wallpaper samples from paint stores, or brochures and maps from travel agencies.

- Visuals unrelated to your lesson are unnecessary and can prove to be very distracting for the learners. Use posters, pictures, decorations, and objects that relate to the goals of the lesson. Use the learners' own artwork as much as possible.

- Involve your learners in arranging the learning space. Don't conduct your lessons from a front desk or table. Use a small table, a lectern, or some other minor piece of furniture to hold your manual, your notes, and other materials.

- It is always important to have the learning space prepared before learners arrive. Be there early enough to have the necessary time to prepare, so you can be present to the learners as they arrive. Have your supplies organized and any equipment you are using ready and in working order.

Do your best with the resources you have, then teach with confidence, joy, and love!

Share your joy in accompanying them on their faith journey. Present loving images of God.

As you end this session

Use your imagination in preparing your teaching space for your next session. Watch TV shows for ideas, especially if you teach children or youth. Refer to your text and other resources such as books and magazines for teachers and catechists. Ask another catechist, teacher, or your catechetical leader for ideas.

> The catechist must consider all the human factors of a particular age level in order to present the Gospel message in a vital and compelling way. **NDC 48**

Catechism connection

In preparing your learning space with care, you create an environment in which your learners may open their minds and hearts to God's loving plan. Read and reflect on articles 50–73 of the *Catechism of the Catholic Church* to explore this in greater depth.

In preparing your learning space with care, you create an environment in which your learners may open their minds and hearts to God's loving plan.

MY THOUGHTS

SESSION

2

Planning *the* learning session

The goal of this session is to highlight the importance of planning and preparing for a lesson.

YOUR OBJECTIVES ARE:

- to learn how to set your goal and objectives
- to learn how to plan effective lessons
- to acquire different strategies for review and application

SKILL: Planning lessons effectively

BEGINNING THIS SESSION

Before you begin to develop your skill in planning lessons effectively, take a few moments for reflection and prayer.

Growing in holiness

Our God is amazingly generous and wants to give us everything with no limits. In fact, God desires our happiness more than we do. God wants us to know the kind of joy that comes only through intimacy. God wants us to grow in holiness and love. There's just one hitch. We've been given the gift of freedom, so we can refuse God. We can close our hearts to the work God desires to do in us. We can block the way to our becoming holy women and men.

At the beginning of his *Spiritual Exercises*, St. Ignatius encourages a person to pray for a generous heart. He understands how important it is to be receptive to God's grace. If we open ourselves, there is no end to the wonders God can and will do in us. God wants us to become holy men and women and to become bearers of the Good News to others. God desires that we grow in faith so that we might become more effective catechists and teachers.

Growing in holiness is not our doing, but rather God's work in us. People do not become saints because of how hard they have tried to be good, but because they have allowed God to take over their lives. We are God's work of art, and God is laboring in our souls to slowly but surely create something amazingly beautiful. When we are generous with God, God can mold us and fashion us into his holy people. Most of our job is just to stay out of the way and not put up walls that keep God out.

Take a moment to reflect

Ask yourself: Do I want God in my life? Do I want God to change me? What am I afraid of? What are some of the ways I resist God?

The time of prayer
End your time of prayer with a prayer for the grace you desire from God. Today, ask for the grace of generosity of mind and heart so that you might be able to receive God's bounty. Begin with the words that follow, and then continue to talk to God in your own words.

Thank you, dear Lord, for your
overwhelming generosity.
You have been so good to me.
I want you in my life. Circle
round me. Enfold me.
Break down my resistance to
your love, gentle God,
and heal the envy of my heart.
Give me a generous spirit, and in everything
help me to trust your love for me.

From personal reflection to sharing faith
As a catechist, you have the opportunity to share God's generous love with your learners. In this session, you will develop skill in planning the learning session in order to create an environment in which your learners may open their minds and hearts to this incredible love of God for us.

TOOLS FOR TEACHING

> The effective presentation of the Christian faith also depends on the methodology employed in the transmission of the Good News. **NDC 26**

Setting the tone
The goals and objectives for the learning experience are often outlined in the catechist's or teacher's manual. But what do they mean to you?

A goal is the main outcome toward which you work as a teacher or catechist. It is the primary aim of a lesson. Objectives describe specifically what knowledge and skills the learners will acquire by the end of the learning experience. The goal and objectives drive your lesson forward. Try to link everything you do in a lesson—presentation, activities, discussions, review—with one or more of the lesson's objectives and, ultimately, with the lesson's goal.

Formulate objectives that are specific, concrete, and measurable, keeping in mind the age, experience, and needs of your learners. For example, look at the goal and objectives for this session. As you read and experience the session, assess how well these objectives are presented and whether you attain them (at least to a degree).

The importance of this session
This section outlines the key elements for a good lesson plan. How do you plan a lesson that is effective and engaging?

- Know your learners.
- Set your goal and objectives.
- Write lesson plans, including creative activities, that reach and motivate your learners.
- Acquire various strategies for review and application.

Well-prepared lessons are a skill and an art. Balance many elements to ensure that your learners are involved in acquiring the knowledge they need, learning how to apply it, and, at the same time, enjoying learning. As the catechist, know the lesson well yourself. The lesson goes from your heart to the hearts of your learners. Know the major points you want them to learn, which activities to use, and when you want to use them.

Keep in mind that your learners are immersed in a culture in which people want to experience life directly—want to participate and interact—in which they look for images and hunger for connection. Your children, youth, and adults bring these expectations to their learning.[2]

2 John Roberto, *Becoming a Church of Lifelong Learners: The Generations of Faith Sourcebook*, Twenty-Third Publications.

Always try to maintain flexibility. Remain open to the Spirit, and don't be afraid to change course somewhat if an important question or situation arises. Allow yourself sufficient time for planning your lesson. Above all, keep in mind the ultimate purpose of lesson planning: to lead your learners to conversion and commitment to Christ and to guide them in their lifelong journey of faith.

Faith is passed on through the witness both of what we do and what we say. It is communicated in our lifestyle and our words. How do you make witnessing to the faith personally a part of your lesson preparation?

Step one: *create effective lesson plans*

This section describes the importance and major stages of good lesson planning. Lesson plans are important for several reasons.

- They challenge you to be prepared. They ensure that your learners absorb what they need to know. They address the individual needs of your learners. They help you make the best use of time. They afford a means to evaluate your teaching.

- You have already learned the purpose of the goal and objectives of a lesson. The next step is to look at the three major stages of effective lesson planning:
  - » a stimulating opening
  - » the development of the lesson
  - » the summary and application

We'll talk about the first two in Step Two, and the assimilation, review, and application in Step Three.

Step two: *develop the lesson*

The opening and development of the lesson are critical in engaging and holding the learners' attention and presenting the message.

OPENING

A stimulating and engaging opening activity is critical to your lesson as the means of stimulating your learners' interest. Refer to your text and manual. Begin with prayer, followed by some form of activity that is age-appropriate and helps learners relate their life experience to the topic of the lesson.

After the opening, there are two more important steps. First, connect the present lesson with the last one. Such a review helps consolidate learning. Then briefly involve learners in an overview of the objectives of the present lesson, using questions, discussion, or an activity.

DEVELOPMENT OF THE LESSON

The heart of the lesson lies in what and how the learners actually learn from the teacher or catechist. Refer to your catechist's or teacher's manual as well as the religion text as a starting point, but do not make these your only resources. Books, magazines, and other materials written for catechists and religion teachers provide concrete ideas and suggestions that you can put into practice.

Plan not only what to teach but the methods you will use to teach it. You want the lesson to "come alive" for your learners so they can experience the message and presence of Christ.

STRATEGIES FOR PRESENTING THE TOPIC

Vary your method of presentation, using one or more of the means suggested here or others you have found effective. Refer also to your manual.

> A stimulating and engaging opening activity is critical to your lesson as the means of stimulating your learners' interest.

- Use the lecture format, in which you share information directly with the learners. Keep lectures brief, with a limited number of concepts, according to the age level of the learners. Lectures that call for the learners' participation or interaction provide a fuller learning experience.

- Use various forms of media, including music (especially contemporary scriptural and liturgical), film, photos, PowerPoint, or some combination of these to help you present the lesson. Prepare the learners beforehand, and follow up with some form of discussion or conclusion.

- Brainstorming, conducting personal interviews and sharing the results, or having learners take part in an event or liturgical celebration (for example, a baptism) are all other methods of presenting and acquiring information.

- Activity centers that engage the different multiple intelligences (see session 4, page 39) strengthen the message by allowing learners to process the information using their strongest form of intelligence.

- Whichever method you choose for sharing the information, weave together the important elements of Scripture, doctrine, liturgy, and witness (Christian living).

Step three: ***assimilate, apply, and review***
You will find a variety of methods for engaging the learners in active discovery.

METHODS

In addition to your presentation of the subject, you should use various methods for engaging the learners in active discovery. These methods must always serve a purpose—to review, to assess how well the learners are absorbing the material, to help them assimilate and apply it, or all three.

ACTIVITIES THAT HELP THE LEARNER SYNTHESIZE THE MATERIAL

- Prepare age-appropriate questions that challenge the learner to think and to apply the lesson to life. Ask open-ended questions, questions that will involve them in discussion and/or require them to make decisions. Give them enough time to think about their answers.
- Faith sharing, that is, sharing one's personal experience and response to a Scripture passage, world event, or story, is an effective means for growth as a Christian and emphasizes the message of the lesson.
- Ask learners to integrate what they have learned by having them connect images with words, think of as many words as they can that relate to the central word, and so on.
- Engage the learners in small group work to discuss what they have learned and what it means to them. Give them the opportunity to explore the subject. (A great tool for this are the activities found in your text and manual.)

ACTIVITIES THAT INVOLVE LEARNERS IN HANDS-ON ACTIONS:

- Use hands-on activities or projects that allow the learners to create objects based on what they have learned, for example, mobiles, drawings, notebooks, posters, collages, murals, dioramas, newspapers, and more. These activities can be carried out by individuals or assigned to small groups.
- Involve young learners in movement: dancing, singing with gestures, games, processions, acting with puppets.
- Older children, youth, high school students, and adults can role play, prepare and act out stories, simulate real-life problem situations, take on creative music or video projects, be engaged in learning-center activities, and take part in educational games, such as a form of Bible trivia.

Prepare age-appropriate questions that challenge the learner to think and to apply the lesson to life.

- For every lesson, intentionally include a variety of different age-appropriate learning methods to enhance the learning experience. After the learners have experienced the subject matter, they will have the opportunity to pull together the information they have received and see it as a whole. In addition, they will be able to use what they have learned in a creative way that engages not only their minds but their feelings and senses—the whole person—as well. Your choice of activities will therefore help them assimilate and apply the knowledge they have gained.

- Review at different points during the lesson. Your learners' abilities to reason and apply material are more likely to be helped by questions such as "How does the sacrament of baptism affect your life today?" or by some form of activity.

- At or near the end of the lesson, summarize the important points. Give the learners the opportunity to summarize also, through one of the types of activities noted above—that is, by synthesizing or by using what they have learned.

As you end this session

Evaluate your last religion session. Think about how your preparation helped you.

> Sound catechetical resources...in the hands of faithful and skilled catechists can be powerful instruments in the proclamation of the Gospel. **NDC 66**

Catechism connection

In planning your learning session with care, you create an environment in which your learners may open their minds and hearts to respond to God's love. Read and reflect on articles 142–184 and 1803–1845 of the *Catechism of the Catholic Church* to explore this in greater depth.

MY THOUGHTS

SESSION

3

Liturgy *as a* teaching moment

The goal of this session is to help you connect liturgy with catechesis.

YOUR OBJECTIVES ARE:

- to learn how to break open the word of God together with your learners
- to learn how to effectively integrate the liturgy into the formation session
- to learn how to use the period of post-baptismal catechesis, or mystagogia, as a time to grow in the understanding of the liturgy

SKILL: Live the liturgy so it will also be an important element of your teaching

BEGINNING THIS SESSION

Before you begin to develop your skills in connecting liturgy with catechesis, take a few moments for reflection and prayer.

Beauty opens the way

Some have said that the experience of beauty is the forgotten key to opening the soul to God. As catechists, we will often focus our efforts on imparting those truths of doctrine and those teachings of Christ that are central to our faith. While these may be important, they don't always lead our students to an experience of God. God remains at most a fascinating idea or a reasonable truth. One can talk forever about God, but until someone experiences the presence of God, they do not really "know" God.

Beauty is like a window into the divine. Just as the soul of any artist is revealed in the art they create, so too the soul of God, the Great Artist, is revealed in the world that is the work of his hands. If we take the time to see the beauty of this world with new eyes, we will be drawn into the heart of the Holy One.

Treasures of great beauty surround us, sometimes forgotten or overlooked as we hurry about our lives. They can be found in physical beauty, in the vitality of youth and the wisdom of age, in the mysteries of science, in acts of justice and forgiveness, in moments of love and intimacy, and even in intense grief. Beauty is not always pretty. While it can be seen in the harmonious lines of a Michelangelo sculpture, it can also be found in the deep furrowed wrinkles of an old woman.

Take a moment to reflect

Ask yourself: How and where do I experience beauty? Do I allow beauty to be a part of my life?

The time of prayer

Close your eyes and for a few moments picture something beautiful that you saw today. Stay with that image and take its goodness into your soul. You don't need to say anything. Just allow your heart to be moved to adoration of the Creator.

When you're ready, continue with the following prayer, or with a prayer in your own words. Speak to God as the child of God that you are, with your heart fully open.

Great and wonderful God,
I stand here in awe before this
beauty you have created.
It is just one reflection of the goodness
and beauty that is yours.
I ask for the grace to open my soul to
the beauty that surrounds me,
often hiding beneath the surface
of things, sometimes missed
because I am moving so fast.
There is so much brutality and
ugliness in this world
and I need to be reminded
that there is goodness and beauty here too.

From personal reflection to sharing faith

As a catechist, you have the opportunity to share the goodness and beauty of God with your learners. In this session, you will develop skill in liturgy as a teaching moment in order to create an environment in which your learners may open their minds and hearts to this incredible love of God for us.

TOOLS FOR TEACHING

> Liturgical catechesis prepares for the sacraments by promoting a deeper understanding and experience of the liturgy. **GDC 71**

Setting the tone

Read and reflect on this passage from St. Cyril's Jerusalem Catechesis: "You were brought to the baptismal font just as Christ was taken down from the cross and placed in the tomb. Each of you was asked, 'Do you believe in the name of the Father and of the Son and of the Holy Spirit?' You made the profession of faith that brings salvation; then you were immersed in the water and three times rose again. This is a symbol of the three days Christ spent in the tomb. When you were immersed in the water, it was as though night had fallen and you could not see in the darkness. But when you came out of the water, it was like coming into the light of day. At that moment you died and were born again. This is an amazing thing! We did not actually die and rise; we only did this symbolically. But we have truly been saved. We share in Christ's passion through symbols and gain salvation in reality. How boundless is Christ's love!" [3]

The Importance of this session

Part two outlines ways of linking liturgy and catechesis.

3 Mystagogy V, from St. Cyril of Jerusalem: Catechesis (Jerusalem Catechesis).

- How do you assist learners in understanding the nature of the liturgy and how it unfolds in the church?
- Break open the word of God together with your learners.
- Find ways to integrate the liturgy into your formation sessions.
- Use mystagogy as a model for your catechesis.

In the liturgy we celebrate the paschal mystery of Christ. When we participate in the liturgy, we take part in the act of worship, but we also commit ourselves to living as the body of Christ, proclaiming the Good News of Jesus and living a life of love. Through the action of the Spirit, liturgy shapes our lives as Christians.

Catechesis and liturgy are closely linked. We can't just "learn about" the mystery of Christ and our faith; we also have to experience it; and we do this in the celebrations of the liturgy.

Step one: ***break open the word***

This section presents Mary as the model for contemplating and applying the word to her life. It describes how you can break open the word with your learners.

"While Mary contemplated everything she had read and heard, she grew even more in faith, wisdom, and charity. The mysteries of God were opened up to her, and joy filled her heart. Her mind was entirely blessed because, through the presence and action of the Spirit, she was always open to the power of God's word. Do as Mary did. Look deep into your heart so you can be cleansed from your sins." [4]

Jesus said, "But as for what was sown on good soil, this is the one who hears the word and understands it, who indeed bears fruit and yields, in one case a hundredfold, in another sixty, and in another thirty" (Mt 13:23). Breaking open the word with your learners entails these steps:

4 St. Lawrence Justinian, Sermon on the Purification of the Blessed Virgin Mary.

- Read the Scripture passage together prayerfully, using a Bible adapted to their age.
- Ask your learners to listen with their hearts.
- Help the learners search for God's word for them and for the community of believers that they can apply to their lives. This is the key to the whole prayerful process.
- If necessary, guide them in reaching a decision to act on what they have shared.

Step two: *link liturgy and catechesis*
Catechesis and liturgy are intimately connected. Catechesis is not just about learning truths; it's about experiencing the mystery of Christ, especially in the ritual activities of the church. We call these rituals the liturgy.

Catechesis prepares persons for the liturgy: Prepare the learners for full, conscious, and active participation in the mystery of the liturgy[5] by teaching them the meaning of the rites and symbols.

Catechesis flows naturally from good liturgy:

- Emphasize the worship and honor of God.
- Help the learners engage the meaning of the rites and rituals of the liturgy.
- Help the learners reflect on their experience of the sacraments and the Sunday liturgy.
- Guide the learners in applying the meaning of the liturgy to their own lives, especially in the call to serve others.
- Liturgy done well is itself living catechesis.
- Review the whole history of salvation as it is celebrated in the sacraments, especially in the Sunday Eucharist through the cycle of the liturgical year. In

5 cf. Constitution on the Sacred Liturgy, 14.

Catechesis is not just about learning truths; it's about experiencing the mystery of Christ, especially in the ritual activities of the church.

the liturgy, we come to know the living God.

- Discover how the truths of faith proclaimed in the Scriptures and the Creed shape your own faith and that of the learners.

- Discuss how the liturgy forms us in a life that is communal, always sending us out in service of our sisters and brothers.

- Employ the music used during the liturgy as another means of catechesis.

THE LITURGICAL YEAR

The essential way in which we as Catholics link liturgy and catechesis is the celebration of the liturgical year. The liturgical year expresses and shapes our Christian identity. It is the celebration of Christ's life throughout the year.

- Follow the ministry, life, passion, death, and resurrection of Christ with the learners as we are immersed in them during the seasons of the church year: Advent, Christmas, Epiphany, Lent, the Triduum, Easter, Pentecost, Ordinary Time.

- On the feast days, holy days, and solemnities, celebrate the mysteries of Jesus and the witness of persons who lived out the paschal mystery.

- Linking liturgy and catechesis is about faith formation and transformation, conversion and discipleship.

Step three: *engage in the mystagogical process in catechesis*

This section discusses mystagogy and its place in catechesis. "Mystagogy" means "guiding into mystery." The word most often refers to the final period of the process of Christian initiation for neophytes, those newly baptized at the Easter Vigil. During the Easter season they and the whole community enter more deeply into the mystery of God's love for us in Christ. Meditation on the Sunday readings and on their experience of the liturgy are two of the principal ways in which neophytes relate the Easter message and mystery to their lives and to their own stories of conversion and transformation. In turn, the neophytes and the community grow in their awareness that as disciples of Jesus we are all called to proclaim God's kingdom.

The process of Christian initiation and, in particular, the time of mystagogy, emphasizes the need for lifelong catechesis. Because we are all in a sense continuing the time of mystagogy (that is post-baptismal catechesis), the elements of mystagogy that serve as a model for catechesis include:

- meditation on the Sunday gospel, especially through faith sharing;
- celebration of the Sunday Eucharist with the community;
- reflection on the experience of the sacraments;
- growth in communion with the members of the faith community;
- the study of Scripture and the liturgy;
- study of the social teachings of the church;
- growth in prayer and acts of charity, especially in works of justice.

STRATEGIES FOR DIFFERENT AGE LEVELS

According to their age level, help learners enter into mystery and understand it at least a little. Teach them about the liturgical year and what each season teaches us about Jesus and about God's love for us.

- Young learners absorb material well through movement, handling objects, singing, and so on. Involve primary-age children in processions, such as one leading to placing the Bible on the prayer table before breaking open the word. Use Bible stories, symbolic objects, liturgical music, gestures, and visuals to help them enter into the mystery of Jesus. Involve them in simple, hands-on, seasonal activities.
- Intermediate-age children like to explore. After obtaining the necessary permissions, take the learners for a tour of the parish church. Help them become familiar and comfortable with each space. Or have them experience a

The essential way in which we as Catholics link liturgy and catechesis is the celebration of the liturgical year.

liturgy, and later revisit it by pointing out the various elements of the experience. Discuss the symbolism of the various liturgical colors.

- Middle school learners like to work in small groups and to do research. For example, they might prepare banners for your parish church or teaching space. They can look up the history of feasts, seasons, and traditions, as well as the development of the liturgy. Let them choose a project they are interested in.

- Invite youth, high school students, adults, and the participants in intergenerational gatherings to form groups as families and individuals. You might have them take part in faith sharing based on the Sunday gospel. Celebrate with them the holy days, solemnities, and particularly the Triduum in meaningful ways. Have them prepare prayer services or rituals for the various seasons. Arrange learning centers with liturgical themes.

As you end this session

As you go through the week, carry the message of the Sunday gospel in your heart and reflect on it.

> In the broader sense, mystagogy represents the Christian's lifelong education and formation in the faith.
>
> **NDC 35D**

Catechism connection

In forming your learners for the liturgy and leading them to be formed by the liturgy, you create an environment in which they may encounter God's love. Read and reflect on articles 1066–1209 of the *Catechism of the Catholic Church* to explore this in greater depth.

MY THOUGHTS

SESSION

4

Applying principles *of* faith development

The goal of this session is to learn about the nature of learning and the principles of faith development theory and multiple intelligences as applied to effective religious education.

YOUR OBJECTIVES ARE:

- to learn how to apply the principles of learning to faith formation
- to acquire various methods to reach each learner
- to learn how to apply the multiple intelligences approach

SKILL: Recognize the ongoing development of each learner and use methods suited to each one

BEGINNING THIS SESSION

Before you begin to develop your skill in applying the principles of faith development, take a few moments for reflection and prayer.

The distortion of beauty

Sin is not pretty, and true evil is horrific. The reality of our world is that sin and evil exist alongside breathtaking goodness and beauty. We would much rather ignore the sin in our lives and anesthetize ourselves to the evil that surrounds us. The grace we seek in this exercise is to "own" the sadness, confusion, and shame that our sins cause. It is not easy to look evil squarely in the eye, to see it for exactly what it is. But we do this with God's strong, reassuring hand on our shoulder, ever reminding us of the power of saving mercy.

This whole world—every animal and human being, the wind and sea, the moon and stars—was created good and beautiful by God. Sin enters this world when we twist and distort that goodness and beauty into something it was never meant to be. For example, power can be used for tremendous good as well as for brutal acts of violence. The wonders of scientific knowledge can be used to save lives or destroy thousands. Terrible things are done every day in the name of love.

We look to Jesus to see how a child of God responds to evil. He does not lash out. He does not repay evil by creating more evil. Rather, Jesus takes the evil into himself, suffers the horror and sadness, and redeems our sin with love. Whenever we experience sin and evil, even our own, our best companion is Jesus the Risen One, who shows us the wounds in his hands and feet, the marks of evil that have been transformed by God's most amazing love.

Take a moment to reflect

Read today's news. Awakened to the sin and to the evil sin causes, let your heart feel the day's events as fully as possible. Imagine what the day would be like if love prevailed.

The time of prayer

Close your eyes and for a few moments imagine yourself in the presence of Jesus, the crucified and risen Lord. Let him show you the marks of his wounds. Speak to him about what is in your heart, in the following words or, better yet, in your own words.

Dearest Savior, I don't like to
think of myself as a sinner.
I want to run from the evil I see
in the world, to ignore it,
and even more, to run from
the sin in my own life.
I don't understand how you can
still love me, and yet you do.
I see how you have embraced my
sin, taken it upon yourself,
and redeemed it with a love that is
beyond what I can fathom.
Please help me to allow the power
of your love to transform me.

From personal reflection to sharing faith

As a catechist, you have the opportunity to share our call to embrace God's goodness with your learners. In this session, you will develop skill in applying principles of development in order to create an environment in which your learners may open their minds and hearts to the incredible love of God for us.

TOOLS FOR TEACHING

> The age and the intellectual development of Christians, their degree of ecclesial and spiritual maturity, and many other personal circumstances must be carefully considered in choosing appropriate methodologies.
> **NDC 29**

Setting the tone

How do you learn best?

- By listening to an explanation?
- By seeing a demonstration?
- By doing the task or acquiring the skill on your own?
- By reflecting on the meaning of the lesson?

The importance of this session

- How do you help learners move from knowing about Christ to an experience of an encounter with Christ?
- Apply the principles of learning to faith formation.
- Apply the multiple intelligences approach—different styles of learning—to faith formation.

- Use various methods to reach each learner.

The core of the human person is mystery. You as catechist or teacher are privileged to encounter that mystery, to encourage and assist in the growth of the person, to help learners make the most of their God-given potential to become persons of faith and lead holy lives.

Learning has three dimensions: knowing, relating, and doing. Very young children are anxious to learn about things; they want to know. But they aren't able to relate one fact to another. As learners grow and develop, they move from just knowing about something to relating to that truth or relating it to other truths. When children reach a certain age they begin to act on what they know, that is, they do something with the truth they learn. When persons move through youth into adulthood their motivation to learn and their choices become, in general, less self-centered, and they are also moved to act for others.

When the dimensions of learning are applied to learning about Christ, learners first encounter Christ. They learn about him, hear stories from the gospel, and experience him in the liturgy and the church. Gradually, they move on to build a relationship with Christ, whom they have come to know. Hopefully, they then choose to follow Christ and carry on his mission.

Step one: *grace builds on nature*

The faith development of learners parallels the levels of human learning. Read this section on your own. If you take part in the group sessions, share your reflections with your group.

Christian educator and scholar James Fowler, having studied the research of Jean Piaget and others, began studying faith development, which parallels the levels of learning. Some simplified points from his works are offered here.[6]

CHILDREN AGES TWO TO SIX OR SEVEN

- These children begin to develop what Fowler calls intuitive faith. The first

6 The works of James Fowler include *Faith Development and Pastoral Care*, Fortress Press; *Stages of Faith*, Harper & Row; and *Weaving the New Creation: Stages of Faith* and the Public Church, HarperCollins.

conscious and concrete images of God form during these early years.

- Imagination plays a great part in their faith development, as does imitation of adults.
- Faith stories can help shape their beliefs and values.
- Concrete symbols, gestures, and rituals help form their understanding of God, even at an unconscious level.

CHILDREN AGES SIX OR SEVEN TO ELEVEN

- Story plays an important role in their faith development. They not only enjoy hearing stories; they like to tell stories, which becomes a way of expressing what they feel and experience and what meaning they give to their experiences.
- Their thinking becomes more literal. They want to know what is really true. They can see that the viewpoint of other people is like or unlike theirs, especially of people they know best.
- Children at this stage are very concerned about what is fair. Their view of God is most often that of a parent or other caregiver who is loving and forgiving but also fair, and who rewards good behavior and punishes bad.

PREADOLESCENTS AND ADOLESCENTS

- These young people have the potential for abstract thought and can reflect more deeply on the meaning of their faith stories and beliefs. Relationships with others, especially their peers, become more and more important to them. The desire for relationships is often extended to God, so as their faith forms, teens feel a longing for a personal relationship with God and a desire to please God.
- As they grow more aware of what others think of them, they seek to meet others' expectations.

Learning has three dimensions: knowing, relating, and doing. Very young children are anxious to learn about things; they want to know.

- At this stage they develop the capability for discipleship and later for stewardship.

YOUNG ADULTS AND ADULTS

- They desire genuine spiritual experiences and answers to their questions about God and life in a language that speaks to their reality. They look for ways to serve others and to work for justice. They want to have connections with a community. They seek guidance in making decisions, especially important life decisions.

Step two: *apply the principles of development*

How can you integrate into your formation sessions your understanding of the faith development of your learners?

- Know the learners you teach, that is, their needs, their wants, their abilities, their weaknesses. See them as individuals, not just as a group. Find ways to meet their needs, build on their abilities, and strengthen their weaknesses.

- Reflect on the stages of faith development described by Fowler. (You may wish to do further reading on them.) Let these help you understand the way learners grasp material, how they make decisions, and how they relate to others.

- Read carefully the section in NDC 48 that applies to the learners you teach. The National Directory for Catechesis provides reflections on the readiness of different age levels and outlines the recommended approach, content, and methodology for each age group.

- Keep in mind the principles of development when you plan your learning experiences, choose your method, or prepare activities that are not in the text or in the catechist's or teacher's manuals.

Step three: *use multiple intelligences*

The theory of multiple intelligences describes the ways different learners absorb ideas.

Believing that IQ testing is very limited as a measure of intelligence, Professor Howard Gardner of Harvard University began to do scientific research on the ways people learn. He discovered several intelligences, centered in different parts of the brain but interconnected. One way of approaching a brief study of these intelligences is to see how our Catholic liturgy engages each of them and how we can use them in our religious education sessions.[7]

The verbal-linguistic intelligence is the most familiar and also the most obvious with regard to the liturgy. The Scripture readings paint wonderful word pictures and offer timeless stories that capture the interest of all word lovers. Learners with this intelligence might rewrite or retell a story, be part of a story, report on a story, pray with a Scripture passage, and so on.

Learners with logical-mathematical intelligence are not only concerned with numbers but also with patterns and logical reasoning. They can be engaged by the logical patterns in the rituals of the liturgy, by the prayers that record the history of salvation, and so on. Activities that build on these elements may be used to enhance their experience of the liturgy and their faith.

Learners with strong musical-rhythmic intelligence can absorb truth through the music used in the liturgy. They also learn through the beauty and rhythm of the words and other sounds as well as the silence that are part of the celebration.

Visual-spatial learners will be attracted by the symbols and gestures used in the liturgy: the bread and wine, the cross, the water, the incense, the sign of peace, as well as the colors used for the liturgical seasons. Use these symbols in your prayer time, and discuss the deeper meaning of these symbols and gestures.

Learners whose strength is bodily-kinesthetic intelligence absorb knowledge especially through movement and their senses. They will become involved in the gestures, postures, smells, and ritual movement of the liturgy.

A strong naturalist intelligence gives the learner a sense of the order and purpose in nature, in their environment, as well as in worship. These learners can appreciate

7 See Bernadette Stankard, *How Each Child Learns: Using Multiple Intelligence in Faith Formation*, Twenty-Third Publications.

How can you integrate into your formation sessions your understanding of the faith development of your learners?

Scripture readings that speak of nature and of the order in the world. They also absorb knowledge through the structure and order of the rituals in our liturgies.

Being quiet and reflective is characteristic of intrapersonal intelligence. These learners internalize what they see and hear. They are able to get inside a Scripture story and look at the reasons for various actions. Use activities that encourage learners to examine their experiences and relationship with God.

Learners with strong interpersonal intelligence learn most from the community aspect of the liturgy. Worshiping with their families, friends, and other people has a strong influence on them. They also enjoy sharing the stories of others; again the Liturgy of the Word is a key element for them. Group work, teamwork, and learning about one another are important activities for these learners.

Finally there are the learners whose strength is existential intelligence. They ask and tackle the big questions: the meaning of life, death, what is evil, who is God. The liturgy, especially the Liturgy of the Word, is all about the big questions. It challenges the learners to grow in their faith. And it comforts them. Prayer rituals, journaling, and activities that give these learners time to explore the questions and God's plan for their lives are all ways to engage and challenge their intelligence.

Always remember that sharing faith is a work of the Spirit. As catechists and teachers, we rely on the grace of God to bring to fruit the seeds we plant in the lives of the learners. Build on the liturgical experiences of the learners in planning, and attend to their experiences of faith as they share them.

As you end this session

During this week pray to know your learners better.

> Individuals develop as human beings and faithful followers of Christ in different ways and according to their own pace. **NDC 48**

Catechism connection

In being mindful of your learners' development, you make it possible for them to come to greater belief in God. Read and reflect on articles 198–231 of the *Catechism of the Catholic Church* to explore this in greater depth.

MY THOUGHTS

SESSION

5

Engaging Scripture effectively

The goal of this session is to help you make Scripture an integral part of your life and also of the lives of those you teach.

YOUR OBJECTIVES ARE:

- to teach learners how to understand the Bible, according to their age level, as a collection of books, presenting it as a library
- to learn methods for teaching about sacred Scripture and using it in sessions
- to help learners love and apply Scripture to their lives

SKILL: Teach learners to make Scripture part of their lives, especially by living its teachings in your own life

BEGINNING THIS SESSION

Before you begin to develop your skill in engaging Scripture effectively, take a few moments for reflection and prayer.

How can this be?

Read Luke 1:26–38, then reflect on the following. Angels just don't appear to people every day, even in Scripture. No matter what form the angel Gabriel took, Mary must have been shocked and more than a little afraid. "You're telling me what? That I'm going to have a son? Listen. Maybe you don't understand. I'm still a virgin." But that doesn't stop the angel from delivering his amazing message. "The power of God's Spirit will do this." Perhaps there's a bit of sarcasm in Mary's voice as she replies, "Oh. OK. Now I understand. I've heard of several virgins who've conceived a child by God's hand." Imagine the twinkle in her eye as she watches the angel's face. "And by the way," continues Gabriel, "your barren cousin Elizabeth is going to have a child too. Nothing is impossible for God."

Nothing is impossible. All her life, Mary had believed that God loved her. Here she was being told impossible things and being asked to trust in that love in a way she never imagined. Love stretches us sometimes and invites us to move beyond what is safe and secure. Mary surely didn't understand what it all meant, and she was surely afraid of what the future might bring, but her response comes from her deepest soul. "My wonderful God, of course I trust you. And I surrender my future to you. If this is what you want, let it be done."

Such surrender is really the basic decision of our spiritual life. Will I trust God or not? Will I surrender my life to God or will I choose to believe that I know better what is best for me?

Take a moment to reflect

Do I trust God's love enough to surrender my life?
What keeps me from giving my heart to God?

The time of prayer
Now close this time of prayer by speaking to God using the prayer given here, or, better yet, in your own words.

Thank you, my great and wonderful God,
for teaching me so gently of your love.
I find encouragement in the thought
that Mary might have struggled
with the angel's message,
and that she might have been
afraid and confused.
Yet I watch her respond so generously to you
and surrender her life to you.
Dear Lord, help me grow in holy freedom
so that I might give myself
to you as Mary does.
Help me to say "yes."

From personal reflection to sharing faith
As a catechist, you have the opportunity to share the impact of saying "yes" to God with your learners. In this session, you will develop skill in engaging Scripture effectively in order to create an environment in which your learners may open their minds and hearts to the incredible love of God for us.

TOOLS FOR TEACHING

> Catechesis must, therefore, lead to "the gradual grasping of the whole truth about the divine plan" by introducing the disciples of Jesus to a knowledge of Tradition and of Scripture. **GDC 85**

Setting the tone
How do you help the children understand the Scripture passage better, according to their age level?

Read to or tell your learners the parable of the good shepherd from the Gospel of Luke, chapter 15, verses 1–7, using a children's Bible with younger children. Ask the children what the shepherd in the story does. Why does he go after the sheep? How does that make the children feel? Let the children glue pieces of cotton onto drawings of sheep, and have them write their names on their sheep to remind them of Jesus' love for them. With younger children you might have a "sheep search": hide figures of sheep around the room. Let the children pretend to be the shepherds and search for them.

The importance of this session
How do you teach learners about the importance of Scripture in their lives?

- Teach them that the Bible is the written word of God and that we should listen with reverence.

- Show them how to read Scripture passages and how to integrate those passages in their daily lives.

- Teach about the Bible in your sessions with methods that are age-appropriate and engage your learners.

- The revealed word of God is the heart and soul of faith formation. Keep a copy of the Bible on your prayer table or station and occasionally hold processions with the Bible to demonstrate reverence and honor for God's word. Using Scripture in your prayer experiences helps familiarize your learners with its words and fosters the practice of linking the Scriptures to their lives. Music is another excellent way to teach Scripture. Songs based on the psalms, the gospels, and other Scripture passages are available for every age. Beyond that, guide the learners in finding the messages and lessons God gives us in the Bible.

Step one: *the Bible is a library*

In order to show learners how to use the Bible, you can compare it to a library, something familiar to most learners. Refer to the section in the learners' text that talks about the Bible (for younger children this may be a very short piece).

- The Bible is made up of seventy-three books. If you look at the contents page of your Bible, you will find that there are many different kinds of books.

- Some contain myths, legends, and parables meant to instruct.

- Others include biblical history and theology, poetry and romance.

- Still other books contain sagas or prayers or visions.

So we can consider the Bible to be a library with many different kinds of books—all inspired by God. You can begin by showing the learners that the Bible is divided into the Old Testament and the New Testament. The Old Testament tells us how God created the world and gradually prepared a people for their salvation. The New Testament describes the life, miracles, and teachings of Jesus, as well as his passion and resurrection. It also relates the story and teachings of the early church. Then, according to the learners' age level, when you use a passage from Scripture as part of the lesson or in an activity, or as part of your prayer, you can show them the section of the Bible it comes from.

Step two: *strategies for teaching*

From prayers to parables, the Bible offers a wealth of inspired reading for you and your learners. Read this section on your own. If you take part in the group sessions, share your reflections with your group.

HOW TO USE THE BIBLE

Primary-age children are developing the skills that allow them to put pieces of knowledge together and to think in concrete concepts. Faith stories help shape their beliefs and values. Stress the teachings of the Old Testament stories and the parables of Jesus with hands-on activities—coloring pages, various kinds of puzzles, cutouts, etc. (whose degree of challenge depends on the age), music about the theme or the characters in the Scripture story, and objects that relate to the story. Make a general timeline to show what place each of the major figures had in the history of the Bible. When you tell stories or read from the children's Bible, point out the general area the story is in.

For intermediate-age children, story also plays an important role, and they want to know what is really true. They are very concerned about what is fair, and this influences their view of God. Stress the stories in the Bible, especially the parables of Jesus and the accounts of his miracles, that speak of God rewarding those who are faithful. Pray with psalms that refer to God as faithful, merciful, and just. Help them look up stories in the Scriptures and act them out. Use Scripture-based word puzzles (crosswords, word searches) for introducing, reinforcing, or reviewing a theme.

Middle school learners are beginning to develop skills that allow them to think abstractly and reflect more deeply on faith stories and their meaning. Engage these learners in faith sharing based on the Sunday readings. Invite them to write or act out contemporary versions of some of the Scripture stories, especially the parables. Their long-

From prayers to parables, the Bible offers a wealth of inspired reading for you and your learners.

ing for relationships is extended to God. Talk about relationships (not necessarily marriage relationships) in the Bible that led the persons closer to God (for example, Abraham and Sarah; Moses and his wife Zipporah; David and Jonathan, his brother by adoption; Elizabeth and Zechariah; Mary and Joseph; Paul and the convert Lydia). Help them find where these examples are located in the Bible.

Because the faith experience of youth and high school students is growing, and their relationship with God is deepening, prayer and service to others become more meaningful. Help them find and read about persons of virtue from Scripture whom they can imitate in those areas. Especially focus on the life of Jesus and the call to discipleship. Encourage them to address the question of their vocation, to listen to the voice of the Spirit. Share with them gospel music and music based on the psalms that is relevant for their age.

Make study of the Scriptures part of a comprehensive faith formation program for adults. Foster faith sharing based on the Sunday readings in small groups, including parish ministry groups, small Christian communities, prayer groups, and so on. Both while studying and while reflecting on the readings, the adults will become more familiar with how to use the Bible.

Step three: *methods for teaching with the Scriptures*

You have many methods at your disposal for using Scripture in your sessions. You can make the Scriptures an important part of your lessons in a variety of ways. These methods may be divided into four main groups: storytelling, activities, applying the message of God's word to daily life, and prayer experiences.

Stories and activities

Stories are popular with every age.

- First and second graders like to listen to the stories of the Bible; choose those they can best relate to. Involve the children in the telling of the story, for example, by having them repeat a name or phrase at specific points or by placing figures on a board as you tell it. Let the children retell the story in their own words, dress up and act it out, or do other activities, such as drawing. These all allow you to evaluate their understanding and help them apply the message.

- Third and fourth graders like to explore. They can work in groups and look up information on their own. Again involve the children in the storytelling in different ways, such as role playing or illustrating the story. Help them connect Scripture to life in concrete ways; for example, by acts of service such as making cards or small gifts for sick children.

- With fifth and sixth graders, you will want to integrate their search for meaning, their growing awareness of right and wrong, and their sense of service to others. In teaching the Scriptures, stress the life and message of Jesus. Give them the opportunity to apply that message to moral situations. For example, invite them to role play a situation. Group work is also effective for this age. You might have the children form small groups and each make a chart of the major events in one of the gospels. Use hands-on activities to teach concepts, such as planting mustard seeds and decorating the pots. Engage their imagination. Let the learners take charge of their activities as much as possible. Encourage them to keep a journal to record their reflections on Scripture.

- Seventh and eighth graders and high school students can think abstractly and are more and more aware of the world outside their own. Peer pressure is a big concern. Offer them role models from Scripture. Use group discussion on the meaning of Scripture passages for their daily lives, even by presenting these passages in contemporary scriptural songs. Pose moral dilemmas they can solve by applying the gospel values. Use more involved hands-on activities, such as crafts and games, that draw on the learners' talents.

- For adults and in intergenerational gatherings, engage the participants in faith sharing based on the Sunday readings. Creatively engage adults and intergenerational groups with activities crafted around scriptural themes.

You have many methods at your disposal for using Scripture in your religion sessions.

PRAYER EXPERIENCES

- Music drawn from Scripture is especially effective with younger children. Strive to create a sense of wonder in their prayer experiences.
- With guidance, older learners are able to offer spontaneous and intercessory prayers based on the Scriptures. Help them relate the prayer experience to their lives. You can let them share in the planning of the prayer. You might have each of them write their own version of a psalm, for example.
- For all ages, develop prayer experiences centered on the Scriptures. Symbols used in connection with the Scripture passages add to the experience; for example, blessing with water for the story of Jesus and the disciples on the water, or a clay jar for the wedding at Cana. At each age level, engage all of the learners in some way in the prayer experience, whether as readers, as a chorus, as a leader, and so on. Rituals are especially meaningful.

As you end this session

During this week take a few minutes each day, if possible, to become more familiar with the Bible.

Catechesis must be permeated with biblical and evangelical thought, spirit, and attitudes through constant use of and reference to the word of God.

NDC 24C

Catechism connection

In engaging Scripture effectively, you help your learners to say "yes" to God. Read and reflect on articles 74–141 of the *Catechism of the Catholic Church* to explore this in greater depth.

MY THOUGHTS

SESSION

6

Building *a* community *of* love

The goal of this session is to facilitate the building of an appropriate community of love among your learners by instilling a sense of respect, order, affirmation, and love for one another.

YOUR OBJECTIVES ARE:

to formulate the rules of good conduct for your religion sessions, with the help of your learners, if possible

to learn about the different factors that might motivate a child to misbehave, and to treat these behavioral issues as Jesus would

to learn ways to foster understanding, respect, communication, and collaboration among your learners

SKILL: Build a community of love among your learners, modeled after the communion of love of the Trinity and the example of Jesus

BEGINNING THIS SESSION

Before you begin to develop your skill in building a community of love, take a few moments for reflection and prayer.

Carry God with you

Prayer is a relationship of our whole being, mind, and heart, with the God who loves us. Just as we surround our human relationships with symbols and rituals that assist us in keeping them alive and healthy, should we not look for ways to do the same to deepen our relationship with God? At our workplace we might keep a photograph of our spouse and children on our desk as a way of keeping them present to us. We might regularly call home at lunchtime to check in and see how things are going. At bedtime we might kiss our children goodnight and say, "I love you." In time, our relationship grows deeper through the attentiveness these habits and rituals enable us to give to the ones we love.

The habit of making God part of the fabric of our lives can be aided significantly by similar symbols and rituals. As we endeavor to become contemplatives in action, we need symbols to remind us. Some carry a rosary or a Sacred Heart medal. Others make sure that there is a crucifix on their wall or a Bible on the nightstand. These kinds of religious symbols become anchor points in our consciousness.

We can also take advantage of the daily rituals of our lives to help us. Things like getting out of bed in the morning, driving to work, sitting down to eat, walking the dog, and doing the dishes can become ritual opportunities to allow God to permeate our consciousness.

Take a moment to reflect

How might I bring God into the routine of my day? What might I do that would help me be more aware of God as I go about my activities?

The time of prayer

For a few minutes close your eyes and imagine God's face before you. Rest in the loving gaze of your God. This is the God who loves you so much more than you know, and who wants to be more a part of your life. When you're ready, end with the following prayer, or better, with a prayer in your own words.

God of my heart,
you know me better than I know myself,
and you understand that my
heart really wants you
to be more a part of my life.
Teach me, Lord, as you would
patiently teach a child,
how to allow you to permeate
my daily activities.
I don't think I yet understand
how much you love me
and want to have me close.
Thank you, Lord,
from the depth of my heart,
for your steadfast, enduring love.

From personal reflection to sharing faith

As a catechist, you have the opportunity to share the ways in which we may make a place for God with your learners. In this session, you will develop skill in building a community of love in order to create an environment in which your learners may open their minds and hearts to the incredible love of God for us.

TOOLS FOR TEACHING

Catechesis prepares the Christian to live in community and to participate actively in the life and mission of the Church. **NDC 20.5**

Setting the tone

Communication and collaboration are essential in building community.

Use an exercise such as this to think about the importance of community. The participants form three groups. Each group is given a box of materials (cloth, different objects, and some paper and pencils). The members of each group will choose a parable to act out, using the materials in the box. However, they won't be allowed to use dialogue in their presentation. Each group, in turn, makes their presentation, and the members of the other groups are to guess what parable is being enacted.

The importance of this session

The comparison of changing "water" into "wine" in the following reflection introduces you to means for achieving positive discipline in your sessions. Read this section on your own. If you take part in the group sessions, share your reflections with your group.

How to facilitate the learners in building a community of love:

- Formulate the rules of good conduct for your sessions.

- Learn about the different factors that might motivate a child to misbehave, and treat each behavioral issue as Jesus would, giving your learners the example of how to treat one another.

- Foster understanding, respect, communication, and collaboration among your learners.

A wise educator, Sr. Maxine Inkel, was once meditating on the gospel story of the wedding at Cana. She had been thinking for days about how to speak to other catechists about the joy of teaching. "It's just a matter of learning from Jesus how to turn the water of potentially negative situations into the wine of joy. Turning water into wine can become a wonderful lifelong habit," she later wrote.[8]

In this session, we will study how we can take the "water" of a child with an attitude, find out what is behind it, and turn it into the "wine" of a child's newfound sense of worth.

Jesus himself said, "I am the vine, you are the branches. Those who abide in me and I in them bear much fruit, because apart from me you can do nothing" (John 15:5). When we bring the wine of love into our religion sessions—the love of the Trinity, the love of Jesus, and our own love for our learners—the Holy Spirit will touch their hearts through us and help form a community of love.

8 *What Would Jesus Do? A Catechist's Guide to Discipline*, Twenty-Third Publications.

Step one: *prepare the soil*

Continuing the metaphor of the good wine, if you want to build communities of love in your religion sessions you need to "prepare the soil" in three ways:

- be prepared, confident of your calling, and desirous of helping your learners encounter Christ (Session 1, Tools for Teaching);

- make your teaching area a sacred space where learners feel comfortable and welcome (Session 2);

- prepare appealing lessons that immerse the learners in a true learning experience that leads them to commitment to Christ (Session 3).

The process of conversion is lifelong, so building a community of love is an ongoing process. Discipleship is a commitment to ongoing growth and development.

Another way of preparing the soil is to set realistic rules about behavior during your sessions. If you don't clearly set limits for your learners, they will try to define them by trial and error. You will want to give the reasons for the rules, stressing especially that you want them all to respect one another and feel safe and secure during your sessions.

Make the rules as simple and as few as possible, and state them in a positive way. For example, instead of saying, "Do not talk while another person is talking," say, "Listen to one another with respect." Whenever possible, involve your learners in establishing the rules and also in deciding on the consequences of not keeping them as well as the reward for keeping them. By doing this you transfer ownership of their behavior to them. You might ask them to sign a covenant in which they agree to observe the rules, and, when appropriate, send home a copy to each of their families.

Step two: *cultivate the vines*

Sometimes children with behavior issues have other underlying problems. Read this section on your own. If you take part in the group sessions, share your reflections with your group.

Most are familiar with the child or youth who is distracted or distracting, one who has an attitude, another who seems totally bored, yet another who likes to be the "class clown," and one who likes to "push your buttons." Sometimes, our best efforts to modify such behavior don't seem to bear much fruit.

This may well be an opportunity to get to know the learners better. Often, disruptive behavior has roots beyond what we can immediately perceive. For example, a learner may be looking for the attention he or she does not receive at home, or may actually be hurting inside because of a situation at home and does not know how to express it. He or she may have a poor self-image and is afraid of being laughed at.

What are some steps you can take to discover whether a learner's behavior is a symptom of some other problem? First of all, of course, pray for those learners who

The process of conversion is lifelong, so building a community of love is an ongoing process.

"act out" in your group. Pray for the gifts of the Spirit to address the situation with compassion and love. Following that, you can try some of these other approaches. Keep in mind to always respect the privacy of the learner. When meeting with a learner, make sure another adult is present or visible.

- Talk with the learner privately, making the meeting as informal as possible so the learner will feel more relaxed. You might start with some words of affirmation, then ask if there is some problem outside of the learning sessions. The learners themselves may not always know what the problem is—but this is a start. You may even note something in their body language or their eyes that hints at feelings below the surface.

- Carefully study the learner's responses in the group—both written and oral. These often furnish clues as to the learner's state of mind and feelings.

- Engage the learner in an activity in which he or she plays an important part. The way the learner relates to the others and the reactions you observe may indicate where there is a problem.

- The lighting or ventilation in the room may be poor, or the learners may be fatigued. The latter problem can be at least partially addressed by giving a brief "time out" for a break. Overactive learners, on the other hand, may require more involvement in activities.

- Discuss what you observe in your religion sessions with your learner's family and ask for their suggestions.

Whatever your manner of engaging this challenge, let it be based on knowledge of, and love for, the learners as unique persons, for whom you are called to be not only leader but, in imitation of Jesus, comforter, companion, healer, someone who empowers and encourages them in their journey.

Step three: *gather the grapes*

A man who took great pride in his lawn once found himself with a large crop of dandelions. He tried every method he knew to get rid of them. Still they plagued him. Finally he wrote to the Department of Agriculture. He enumerated all the things he had tried and closed his letter with the question: "What shall I do now?"

In due course the reply came: "We suggest you learn to love them."

In your religion sessions, teach and foster certain qualities in your learners that will allow learning to flourish more easily because a community of love is established. The community won't be perfect, but it will be in process. The qualities are understanding, respect, communication, and collaboration.

- Understanding is the first step or building block. When learners are taught to understand one another and to appreciate each other's differences as gifts, they are less inclined to hurt others or to have problems in relationships. They become less self-centered and their perspective is widened.

- Respect is based on understanding. As learners expect to receive respect, so must they be willing to freely give it. Young learners especially, that is, children and teens, often are not shown this respect in other areas of their lives. Respect helps build up their self-image and esteem and makes them realize their worth as children of God.

- As respect grows, so does the desire and even the need to communicate, especially for young adolescents, youth, and high school students, for whom relationships are becoming more and more important. Encourage them to express themselves freely but also with respect for the feelings and viewpoints of others.

- Collaboration is an important skill for building a community of love. Learning how to work together is essential if the learners are to fulfill their calling as disciples of Jesus to carry on his mission.

- Do your best to foster the above and other qualities in your learners and offer the example of Jesus, and you and your learners will be united with the true vine of the Master.

Respect is based on understanding. As learners expect to receive respect, so must they be willing to freely give it.

STRATEGIES FOR FOSTERING A COMMUNITY OF LOVE

Help learners develop a community of love by using these and similar methods.

- Discuss the learners' experience of the diversity of people coming together to celebrate Eucharist, which can be a model for them. In the Sunday assembly they see the collaboration necessary for a celebration that is reverent and that promotes the "full, conscious, and active" participation of those present: the collaboration of the pastor or presider, the lectors, the ministers of the Eucharist, the altar servers, the music ministers, the ministers of hospitality, and finally the members of the assembly itself. Such collaboration requires respect and understanding as well as good communication within each group and among the groups.

How do you foster a community of love among your learners?

- Find and share with your learners (or have them look up) passages in the gospels in which Jesus taught or demonstrated each of the qualities of a community of love. You will also find such passages in St. Paul's letters and in other New Testament writings. You can make these passages the basis for faith sharing, a prayer experience, role playing, music, or activities. Examples of such passages are found in Matthew 10:40–42 (understanding, respect); 10:1–14 (communication and collaboration); 5:43–48 (respect, love); Luke 5:17–26 (respect); 6:27–36 (respect, understanding, love); 6:37–42 (understanding, respect); 9:10–17 (collaboration); 15:11–32 (respect, understanding, collaboration); John 4:1–15 (respect, understanding, communication); 8:1–11 (respect, understanding, communication).

- Role play with the older learners. Have them act out what they would do in different situations requiring one or more of the four qualities. For example, what would they do if a new person joined their class, if they met someone of a different cultural or ethnic background, if they wanted to express a different opinion on some issue, if someone tried to start an argument with them, if they had to work with someone they didn't like, if someone took something that belonged to them, and so on.

- Involve your learners in group work—according to their age level—that requires communication and collaboration to accomplish a task, for example, the preparation of a prayer service or, for young learners, a certain type of game or other activity.

- Invite learners—again according to age level—to plan together and carry out some form of service or outreach activity.

- As noted above, involve your learners in formulating and enforcing the basic rules of behavior, as well as the rewards or consequences.

As you end this session

Be aware this week of opportunities to build a community of love—at home, at work, with friends.

> The Christian community is the origin, locus and goal of catechesis. **GDC 254**

Catechism connection

In creating a community of love, you create an environment in which your learners may open their minds and hearts to carry God with them throughout their lives. Read and reflect on articles 232–267 and 1877–1948 of the *Catechism of the Catholic Church* to explore this in greater depth.

In creating a community of love, you create an environment in which your learners may open their minds and hearts to carry God with them throughout their lives.

MY THOUGHTS

SESSION

7

Making your lessons visual *and* active

The goal of this session is to help you learn when and how to use such visual aids effectively in your religion sessions.

YOUR OBJECTIVES ARE:

- to learn about various symbols and gestures that lead learners into the mystery of Christ
- to become familiar with the different types of visual aids available for catechesis
- to learn strategies for making the most of such aids

SKILL: Choose and use appropriate visual aids to stimulate the attention and imagination of learners

BEGINNING THIS SESSION

Before you begin to develop your skill in making your lesson visual and active, take a few moments for reflection and prayer.

Your faith has saved you

Read Luke 7:36–50; then reflect on the following: Jesus' reaction to the woman is startling and unexpected by those gathered in the room. He is so tender with her. In an amazingly kind gesture of compassion, he shifts the focus away from the woman and toward the Pharisee who questions his actions. Surprisingly, he doesn't chastise the woman for her sinfulness, but rather, he chastises the Pharisee for his arrogance in judging her actions and judging Jesus himself for receiving her act of contrition. Sometimes we hear the voice of the Pharisee in our hearts because we just can't understand a God who is so generous with his mercy.

Jesus reveals in this story the heart of God. God never spurns us or abandons us. Without hesitation God welcomes us and holds us in the arms of his mercy. It's not important to God that we count our sins or enumerate the details of our sinfulness. The hardest part is for us to overcome our shame and turn to God for forgiveness. We find it hard to believe that God still loves us, even in our sin. We, not God, are the ones who separate ourselves from his love. All we have to do is be ready to receive the unconditional love that's waiting for us.

Holiness is something akin to standing naked and ashamed before God and looking into the eyes of his love. It is that unbounded love, rather than our own efforts, that will transform us from sinner to saint. The glory of our goodness comes from God, not from ourselves. Our joy is indeed great because we are beloved sinners.

Take a moment to reflect

Ask yourself: What area of sinfulness do I allow to separate myself from God? Of what am I most ashamed? Is there anything that I have a hard time believing that God would forgive?

The time of prayer
As in previous exercises, we now end our time of reflection with a colloquy, a heartfelt prayer, in one's own words. This should be like a friend talking to a friend. Begin with the words provided below, and then continue as your heart moves you. Ask God for what you desire.

Dearest, most merciful Jesus,
I am overwhelmed with the depth
of your love for me.
Sometimes I stay away because
it's hard for me to believe
that you would welcome me in my sin.
Forgive my arrogance in not
trusting your love.
I'm so grateful, Lord, that you've
welcomed me home.
Let me never judge my brothers and sisters,
but may I always be ready to
embrace them in forgiveness
and extend to them the abundance
of your mercy.

From personal reflection to sharing faith
As a catechist, you have the opportunity to share the transforming love of God with your learners. In this session, you will develop skill in making your lessons visual and active in order to create an environment in which your learners may open their minds and hearts to this incredible love of God for us.

TOOLS FOR TEACHING

> Catechetical aids...that are faithful to God's Revelation...can be very effective in the hands of skilled catechists. **NDC 71**

Setting the tone
This experience introduces the topic of utilizing visual media to engage the learners.

Read Jesus' teaching about "Do not worry....Look at the birds of the air....Consider the lilies of the field....Strive first for the kingdom of God" (Matthew 6:25–33). Decide what visuals from this passage you could incorporate in your faith-formation sessions.

The importance of this session
This section describes some of the visuals Jesus used to teach his message. As educators you can follow his example.

How can you use visual media to stimulate the attention and imagination of learners?

- Learn about symbols and gestures that lead learners into the mystery of Christ.
- Become familiar with the different types of visual aids and activities available for catechesis.
- Learn strategies for making the most of them.
- Images have been around as long as stories have—in fact, the first stories were told in pictures. Even today, some

written languages are based on or are forms of "pictures" (e.g., Chinese, Japanese).

Jesus made good use of concrete images when he taught. He changed the water into wine at the wedding in Cana and so began his public ministry (John 2:11). He used the water in a well to teach the Samaritan woman that he is the living water (John 4:10). He compared the disciples to salt and light (Matthew 5:13–14); he pointed to the birds of the air and the lilies of the field (Matthew 6:26–28). He multiplied the loaves and fish to feed the crowd but also as a sign that he was the bread of life (John 6:35). He used mud to restore the sight of a blind man (John 9:6–7), then spoke of spiritual blindness (John 9:39–41).

Jesus blessed the children and said, "For it is to such as these that the kingdom of heaven belongs" (Matthew 19:14). And just as he had allowed John to baptize him in the river (Matthew 3:13–17), he allowed a woman to anoint him in preparation for burial (Matthew 26:12).

In the mystery of his passion, death, and resurrection, Jesus gave the ultimate explanation of what he had come to earth for. In his moments of suffering, and without words, he taught mercy, forgiveness, patience, and above all, love.

Step one: *use symbols and gestures*

Catholic liturgy and tradition offer a rich variety of symbols and gestures to help capture the imagination and enhance the understanding of learners. The church's liturgy abounds with symbols and gestures that can be used not only for prayer but also to illustrate a gospel passage, a story, or an aspect of the faith. Some of these symbols and their meanings are given below.

- Bread: nourishment, Jesus the bread of life, Eucharist, meal, sharing, communion

- Wine/grapes: health, sacrifice, Blood of Jesus, fruit of the earth, Eucharist, Jesus the vine, communion

- Water: new life, cleansing, living water, quenching thirst, baptism

- Oil: anointing, healing, appointed to service, strengthening
- Cross: faith, Jesus' sacrifice, witness, blessing
- Candle: light of faith, Jesus the light, expectation, prayer
- The altar: the table of sacrifice, of the Eucharistic meal we share, of unity
- Incense: prayer, adoration, blessing, purification
- Bible: word of God, our faith, God's presence
- Colors: purple (penitence, royal); white (purity, joy, new life); red (the Spirit, blood of Jesus and of the martyrs, witness, love); green (hope, life); gold (celebration, joy)
- Laying on of hands: healing, service, invoking the Spirit, blessing

Other symbols represent God.

- Father: Creator, Pillar of Fire, Cloud, Light
- Son: Jesus, Son of God; Savior
- Fish: the Eucharist
- Shepherd: the one who cares for us
- Crown: Jesus the king; Chi-Rho: first two letters of Christos; IHS: Jesus, Savior; lamb: the sacrifice and victory of Jesus
- Holy Spirit: Wind, breath, dove: sanctifying power, tongues of fire: Pentecost, love, mission (both images taken from Scripture)

Symbols used in catechesis enrich the learners' understanding of the faith and provide multi-layered, visual "insights" into the mystery of Christ and of the Trinity.

Step two: ***show and tell***

The visual media and activities available are so numerous that we can only provide

Symbols used in catechesis enrich the learners' understanding of the faith.

a partial listing here. You have a rich variety of visuals to choose from to spark learners' imagination and interest. Interactivity is the key. As often as possible, let learners work together on a project.

VISUALS IN THE TEXTS. Most religion texts include pictures and other visual aids related to the lesson. Discuss and refer to them as you present the message. Let older learners discuss them in small groups.

VISUALS ON DISPLAY. These convey a story or message with a few words and/or pictures. They include posters, murals, collages (images and words overlapping each other), banners (can be made of paper, fabric, a branch, paper bags, embroidered, or made in the form of a kite), large pictures, and signs. Decorate your meeting space to fit the theme in a creative way, using simple, accessible objects.

BOARDS. Various types of boards can involve learners in more active ways. Felt boards with felt figures can be used to engage learners in a story. Paper "boards" and easels offer the means for drawing pictures and rebuses. Poster boards and bulletin boards can be used to hang pictures or signs that accompany the lesson or story.

GAMES. Games are excellent for helping learners review, assimilate, and apply a lesson, as long as you do not make them ends in themselves. These include crossword puzzles and word searches, rebuses, mazes, board games, relays with objects related to the lesson, Bible (or other faith topic) charades, and adaptations of popular TV game shows.

ARTS, CRAFTS, EXPERIMENTS. These allow the learners to express their own understanding of the lesson. Some arts and crafts are: drawing; painting; making figures and objects out of paper, modeling clay, papier-mâché, felt, pipe cleaners, fabric, wallpaper samples, etc. Learners can make cards for different occasions, dioramas (scenes in a box or other container), terrariums, candles (under adult supervision only), Advent wreaths or calendars, and class or individual scrapbooks. Other activities include making bookmarks with quotes from the Bible or the saints, maps of the Bible lands, timelines, and charts. You can have the learners carry out simple science experiments to illustrate a point about the lesson, for example, making sugar crystals to show God's impact on our lives, or having them "analyze" their spiritual DNA.

PUPPETS. Puppets are an engaging way to let learners retell a story or review a lesson. They can be very simple, such as finger puppets; stick puppets made of construction paper, soft foam board, or paper plates glued to popsicle sticks or dowels; or sock puppets with faces drawn on, yarn for hair, and a piece of fabric for clothing.

DRAMA. Drama assumes many forms and provides a fun way to review and assimilate. Acting out the story, with or without dressing up; doing a dramatic or choral reading; role playing a situation; and miming (acting without words) are all ways to actively involve the learners. Formulate mystery stories using fictional or real characters and/or situations (for example, ask "What do you think happened to Noah's ark?").

Each of these types of visuals has numerous variations that offer a wide variety of aids to enrich the message you are imparting.

Step three: *engage your learners*

How can you use the symbols and visuals you just read about in a practical way? Some suggestions follow, and you'll certainly discover others.

PRIMARY-AGE LEARNERS

- Pour water from a pitcher into a bowl. Let the children dip their hands in the water. Refer to your text about baptism.
- Have each child draw faces on paper plates and hold them up as you read one of the parables to them, e.g., the good Samaritan.
- To talk about new life, show the children how to make butterflies out of wallpaper samples and pipe cleaners. Then discuss why the butterfly is a symbol for new life.

How can you use the symbols and visuals you just read about in a practical way?

- Build a "maze" for the children to go through, using signs with clues, and at the end have an object related to your lesson.

INTERMEDIATE-AGE LEARNERS

- Invite the children to make a mural or large poster with the symbols linked to the celebration of the Eucharist. Or you could have them work in groups, each group making its own poster.
- Ask the children to each make a shoebox diorama of one of the parables of Jesus.
- Play Bible charades to review a story from the Scripture that was part of your lesson.

FOR MIDDLE SCHOOL LEARNERS, YOUTH, AND HIGH SCHOOL LEARNERS

- Ask them to each make a banner representing his or her name-saint, including the symbol for the saint. The banner can also illustrate an episode from the life of the saint.
- Have learners form small groups. Assign each group a theme related to a recent lesson, and ask each to compose a word search containing ten words related to that lesson.
- Invite learners to form small groups. Each group is to mime a scene illustrating a virtue or one of the commandments. The others have to guess which sacrament (or virtue or commandment) is being depicted.

FOR ADULTS OR INTERGENERATIONAL GATHERINGS

- Have each family work together (or individuals on their own) to make a family tree. You will need some small tree branches, disposable cups or cans with lids removed, clay, green paper, scissors, glue, and markers.
- Tell a story to the whole gathering (perhaps having different persons reading different parts). Then in the small groups, invite the children to retell the story to the adults, using whatever visuals they choose.
- Go to the internet for free Bible maps you can copy. Choose the map of Palestine at the time of Jesus or the ministry of Jesus. Make a list of the main cities and the events that took place there (give Bible citations). Have the groups find the cities and look up the citations. For example, Bethlehem (Luke 2:1–7), Nazareth (Luke 1:26–27), Cana (John 2:1–2), Capernaum (John 2:12), Sychar (John 4:1–6), Jerusalem (Luke 2:41), Bethany (John 11:1–2), Emmaus (Luke 24:13–14).

As you end this session

Look for the symbols in your life that have special meaning for you in your relationship with God and with others.

> In his teaching Jesus made use of "all the resources of interpersonal communication, such as word, silence, metaphor, image, example, and many diverse signs." **GDC 140**

Catechism connection

In making your lessons visual and active, you create an environment in which your learners will grow as disciples of Jesus Christ. Read and reflect on articles 557–570 and 595–682 of the *Catechism of the Catholic Church* to explore this in greater depth.

In making your lessons visual and active, you create an environment in which your learners will grow as disciples of Jesus Christ.

MY THOUGHTS

SESSION

8

Moving *from* experience *to* faith

The goal of this session is to explore how we can best engage the life experiences of our learners to help them grow in faith, in conversion, and in commitment to Christ.

YOUR OBJECTIVES ARE:

- to help learners move from life experiences to better knowledge of themselves and of God (following Jesus' example in using experience in his teaching); in turn, faith will shed light on their experiences
- to teach learners that sinful experiences can lead them away from God
- to learn how to organize the teaching space

SKILL: to learn methods for incorporating the life experiences of learners in your sessions

BEGINNING THIS SESSION

Before you begin to develop your skill in moving from experience to faith, take a few moments for reflection and prayer.

God with us

Sometimes the hardest part of the story of Jesus' birth is its familiarity. The act of God taking human flesh is an act of intimacy. It is a story of a God who is so in love with us that we can barely fathom it. We feel uncomfortable with this kind of closeness to God because we feel unworthy. Furthermore, to speak of God in such human terms can seem inappropriate, if not blasphemous. And yet this is what we Christians do. The infinite, all perfect God is presented to us as a human infant, born in a lowly cattle stall to poor parents of no great importance. Such is the foolishness of God's wisdom!

In the person of Jesus, spirit and matter are at once united. The divine permeates the universe of material things in such a way that the created world is set on a course of becoming more and more divine. As the divine God takes on our humanity, so our humanity begins to take on more and more of God's divinity. The work and power of God's redemption of this world is set in place. To those who see with the eyes of faith, God continues to take flesh for us in thousands of unexpected ways and faces. This is what Ignatius of Loyola in his Spiritual Exercises calls "finding God in all things."

Take a moment to reflect

Ask yourself: Where do I find the face of Christ?

The time of prayer

The grace of contemplation is deepened when we take the images and persons of our prayer with us into our daily lives. So, as you go through your week, remember what you experienced in your time of prayer. Let the words and images be with you as you work, play, study, eat, and pray.

Great and infinite God,
your desire to be close to humanity
overwhelms me.
Why would you even want
to bother with us?
I kneel beside the manger crib
to see this tiny infant,
the beauty of God in the flesh,
so simple, so divine.
My heart sometimes doesn't know
how to take it all in,
and with Mary I try to hold it all
in the quiet of my heart.
Dear Lord, give me the eyes of faith
so that I might recognize you
whenever and wherever you
take flesh for me.

From personal reflection to sharing faith

As a catechist, you have the opportunity to share God's desire to be close to humanity with your learners. In this session, you will develop skill in moving from experience to faith in order to create an environment in which your learners may open their minds and hearts to this incredible love of God for us.

TOOLS FOR TEACHING:

Catechesis helps people relate the Christian message to the most profound questions in life. **NDC 29A**

Setting the tone

This exercise gives you an example of how you can use a life experience in your religion sessions. Ask your learners to imagine the following scene.

You are having a special Sunday meal together because a relative has come for a visit. What kinds of food might your family prepare? Will you decorate the table and the room? Do you invite other relatives to your meal? With what other customs does your family celebrate special occasions?

How is celebrating the Eucharist like a special family meal? What makes it different?

The importance of this session

How can you help learners link their daily experiences with their faith life?

- Lead learners from their experiences to a better knowledge of themselves and of God, following Jesus' example in using experience in his teaching. Also show them how faith sheds light on their experiences.

- Illustrate for the learners how poor

choices can lead to negative experiences that can lead us away from God.

- Learn methods for incorporating the life experiences of learners in your sessions.

Children often surprise us with the insights they glean from experience, insights that can be profound and at the same time humorous. For example, once a catechist was reviewing with her children the lesson they had studied the week before about God being all-powerful. The catechist asked, "Is there anything God can't do?"

There was silence. Finally, one boy held up his hand. The catechist was disappointed because she thought the point of the lesson had been missed.

"All right, Kevin," she said resignedly, "just what is it that God can't do?"

"Well," the boy replied, "God can't please everybody."

As catechists and teachers we recognize the need to relate our own personal experiences to our faith and to our relationship with God. So, too, we foster the same awareness in our learners. It is important that we encourage learners to connect faith with life and life with faith. We don't learn about God in a vacuum. Rather, in our search for ultimate meaning in our lives, in seeking to understand better who God is for us, we bring the wisdom of our faith to shed its light on our searching. This searching is filled with the joys and sorrows, pleasure, and traumas of our lives. It is filled with positive and negative experiences, the good and the poor choices of our daily lives. It is in making our way through life that we raise questions about the meaning of our existence, about good and evil in the world, and so on. Jesus knew how important experience was in teaching about the kingdom, about God, and about the life he came to share with us, the life that is the Father's will for all people. When we reflect on the teachings and parables of Jesus, we find constant references to the life experience of the people of his time.

Step one: *experience and faith*

Jesus used the experiences of his listeners to teach them about the kingdom. Remember the movie *Pay it Forward*? Haley Joel Osment plays the role of a young boy being raised by a single mom (played by Helen Hunt). He is influenced by his teacher (played by Kevin

Spacey) to come up with a project that would make a difference in the lives of people. The project involves anticipating people's good and choosing to reach out and help them before they do anything to deserve such help. The film reminds us of many gospel stories about seeds—the gospel of faith the size of a mustard seed, the gospel of seeds planted and growing without our awareness or attention.

Encourage the learners to move from experience to faith. Have them consider their own life experiences in relation to the gospels. Jesus used very down-to-earth images: water, salt, fig trees, a vineyard, a dissolute son, a shepherd. With these examples and others, he helped people find God in their own experiences, to see God in the smallest events and elements of their lives. And he used these experiences to prepare their minds and hearts for belief in him and in his message of conversion, love, and salvation.

Jesus taught about hope and love in the parable of the good Samaritan (Luke 10:29–37). He taught about the meaning of life in the Sermon on the Mount (Matthew 5–7) and in the description of the final judgment, when he rewards those who fed the hungry and gave drink to the thirsty (Matthew 25:31–46).

Invite the learners to memorize facts about the faith, to learn the Creed, and to know their prayer formulas. Remind them that if they do not make what they learn about the faith come alive in their own daily lives, these facts will not help them become disciples of Jesus.

When we see a rainbow or any beautiful thing, we're apt to cry out, "There's God!" We feel God at those moments and can say it. Help your learners find God in the "rainbows."

Step two: *turning away from God*

Because we are free to choose, we can experience sin also. A part of our human experience is to sense the temptation to "the dark side," sin. Discuss with your learners how deep disappointments, loss, serious injury—even more than the weaknesses in our nature—can be occasions for us to turn away from God, from our relationship with God. And because we are free beings, we can make that choice. We can choose to live without God, to live without love for others, while we seek our own satisfaction.

> It is important that we encourage learners to connect faith with life and life with faith.

Our participation in the liturgy of the church, especially the sacraments of baptism, Eucharist, and reconciliation, helps us recognize our weakness and at the same time strengthens our resolve to choose the path to conversion—with the help of the prayers of the community and the grace of God. Still, we may struggle with the "shadow side" of our lives. Jesus spoke of this experience in parables too. In fact, in the well-known parable of the prodigal son, we read about the experience of a young man who chooses to leave his family to pursue a life of pleasure and selfishness. As is the experience of many people who feel that they have "hit bottom" and then look closely at their lives, it is only when the son runs out of money that he realizes his error and repents. He begins his journey back to a father who has already forgiven him.

Use examples from Scripture to illustrate for your learners the power of freedom and the effects of making wrong choices. You can also share how wrong experiences lead to errors in judgment and in choices. The young man in the parable, for instance, may have been influenced by the example of others. Through stories from Scripture like the prodigal son parable, combined with reflections on their own experiences, you can help learners realize that even if they turn away from God, God does not turn away from them. God always loves them and offers the grace of conversion.

Step three: *faith is a verb*

Examining how Jesus used experience has already given you some ideas about how learners' experiences can be a catalyst for their growth in faith. You want your learners to know—in every pore of their body, through every sense they are blessed with—that God, that Jesus, and that faith are real. The following suggestions offer further opportunities.

- Begin from the actual experience of the learners. Set up a scenario, as we did in Step one, and ask questions. Bring in an object and ask if the object reminds them of any experiences they have had. Ask them to draw a picture of a certain type of experience and talk about it. Invite them to list qualities they admire in a person and why. Begin with the experience of a prayer ritual. Talk about their experience of a rite or ritual in the liturgy. Ask them to share special seasonal observances or traditions in their families. Let the learners talk about something that happened to them during the week, making sure they don't speak of matters that are confidential or too personal. Then connect these experiences to the topic you are going to teach. Or, in the case of the last method, help them find God's presence in those experiences, and then relate their experience to the topic.

- Use appropriate activities that engage learners' imaginations and, mindful of the principles of multiple intelligences that we studied in Session 4, engage as many of their senses as possible. Read or let your learners read a story from Scripture or a story from children's literature. Find out through discussion how they relate to it. Have them role play the story, retell it, or use puppets or figures to act it out. Invite them to illustrate the story or write a poem on the topic. Sing a song, possibly with gestures, related to it. Play a game. Engage them in a simple craft that helps them learn about the topic. Then move from these experiences into the topic of your session.

- Let learners pray over a recent event, happy or tragic; then invite them to reflect on the meaning of it. Their prayer can be about something that happened to one of them, or an event in the neighborhood, country, or world.

- According to their age level, invite learners to be involved in acts of service. They can then reflect on the experience and what it meant for them.

- Use different forms of prayer, and help learners become accustomed to reflection. If they are old enough, they can prepare and lead the prayer themselves. Again, engage as many of the senses as possible.

- With older learners, pose moral dilemmas appropriate for their age level. Invite them to discuss it in small groups, role play the situation, or journal about

Use different forms of prayer,
and help learners become accustomed
to reflection.

it, asking themselves what the gospel says about such a choice. Encourage them to provide examples, being careful again that they preserve confidentiality.

Whatever methods you use, you are aiming for your learners to experience a kind of revelation, for them to have a warm, alive, and creative knowledge of God, of their faith, and of their commitment to Christ.

STRATEGIES FOR DIFFERENT AGE LEVELS

Learners of every age enjoy experiencing new things. You can use this to lead them to reflect on faith topics. Refer also to their text and your manual.

- Engage primary-age children in storytelling with motion. For example, play "Follow the Leader" to a Bible story, perhaps the story of Noah's ark. Then draw out the faith message as it relates to their lives. Use activity centers with objects related to different themes or teachings of the faith. Pray together about a recent event that has affected them directly or a tragedy that has affected the lives of many people.

- Invite intermediate-age learners to talk about a new or enjoyable experience they had during the week. Help them relate it to an area of Catholic faith or practice. Read an age-appropriate story or show a short video clip, and ask the children to put themselves in the place of the characters. What would they have done?

- Ask middle school learners to share in groups what they think about a particular new computer game. Does it reflect or go against gospel values? Ask them to tell the stories about their own experiences related to a faith topic. Invite them to work in groups and think about a situation when their peer group might try to pressure them to do something they know is wrong (smoke, take drugs, steal, cheat on an exam). Have them role play the situation with alternative endings.

- Invite youth, high school students, adults, or members of an intergenerational gathering to discuss in groups their experience of a new film or music CD. What are the messages it conveys? Are these in accord with or counter to the gospel? Ask them to come up with a slogan or even a song that conveys the message of one of the gospel parables or teachings. Have them keep track of or estimate how much time their family spends together. What are some things families can do together to celebrate their faith?

As you end this session

During the week, reflect on and write about experiences that caused you to question or to grow or to seek God in your faith.

> Jesus consistently used the ordinary human experiences of daily life to form his disciples. **NDC 29A**

Catechism connection

In moving from experience to faith, you show your learners that God is always with us and that we are created to be close to Christ. Read and reflect on articles 374–421 and 1691–1748 of the *Catechism of the Catholic Church* to explore this in greater depth.

In moving from experience to faith, you show your learners that God is always with us and that we are created to be close to Christ.

MY THOUGHTS

SESSION

9

Teaching *with* faith sharing

The goal of this session is to help you learn to use faith sharing as a teaching method.

YOUR OBJECTIVES ARE:

- to grasp the dos and don'ts in leading faith sharing
- to learn how to use examples of faith as a basis for faith sharing
- to learn how to use questions to engage learners in faith sharing

SKILL: Engage learners in faith sharing

BEGINNING THIS SESSION

Before you begin to develop your skill in teaching with faith sharing, take a few moments for reflection and prayer.

Listening with our hearts

Read Matthew 5:1–12; then reflect on the following. We can imagine Jesus looking out at the faces of these people, asking himself, "What do their hearts need to hear?" He can see their ache and longing, their deep-down hunger for God, their pain. Many of them are troubled souls that are empty of hope. Some are in mourning over the death of a loved one or a deep disappointment. There are those who have been deeply hurt by those who've judged them to be unfit, unacceptable, and unworthy of love.

And so Jesus begins to speak to their souls and tells them that all this ache and longing makes a person blessed. Many of them probably expected him to preach about what they need to do to become holy. But he surprises them by telling them that they're already holy and blessed in God's eyes. What a message of hope and freedom this is! Holiness is not about how many prayers I say or how generous I am. It's about being loved and embraced in one's poverty, meekness, and hunger. It's about being pure of heart and a herald of peace. And it's about one's willingness to bear insult and rejection for the sake of God's kingdom. This is truly good news.

We might find ourselves resisting some of the things we hear in Jesus' teaching. This is a radical new way of thinking and of looking at life. Are we ready to embrace the mind of Jesus, our friend and brother? Like some of the disciples, we may be thinking that this man has to get a more realistic grasp of life. How could he really be serious to count anyone fortunate and blessed who is grieving, meek, or persecuted? Maybe we have a hard time imagining ourselves as poor, meek, or pure of heart.

Take a moment to reflect

Ask yourself: What in Jesus' teaching do I resist? What seems out of sync with my view of the world?

The time of prayer
Now take some time to speak to God using the prayer given here, or, better yet, pray in your own words.

Dearest Lord Jesus,
I come to love and admire you
more and more each day.
I don't always understand your words
but I feel great comfort and freedom in them.
You remind me that I don't have
to earn God's blessing
but that holiness lies in being
myself before God.
Help me, Lord, to see myself as you see me.
I often feel that I am not yet
ready to be your disciple,
yet you call me to your side.
Help me to respond with all my heart.

From personal reflection to sharing faith
As a catechist, you have the opportunity to share the blessing of being close to God with your learners. In this session, you will develop skill in teaching with faith sharing in order to create an environment in which your learners may open their minds and hearts to this incredible love of God for us.

TOOLS FOR TEACHING

> Catechesis rooted in Sacred Scripture should bring about the discovery of the divine truth it contains and evoke as generous a response as possible. **NDC 67A**

Setting the tone
An American teacher, a Christian, was employed in Japan on the understanding that during school hours he should not utter a word on the subject of Christianity. The engagement was faithfully kept. He lived among his students as an example of the Christian life but never spoke of it to them. However, so beautiful was his character and so blameless his example, that, unknown to him, forty of his students met and decided to join him in his faith.[9]

Just as God did through that teacher, God prepares the hearts of learners through you to grow in faith and love for Jesus Christ, to lead them to intimacy with him. You are a messenger of God, sent to light other candles.

The importance of this session
How do you use faith sharing as a teaching method?

- Grasp the dos and don'ts in leading faith sharing.
- Learn how to use stories from our faith

9 Anthony Castle, *More Quips, Quotes, and Anecdotes*, Twenty-Third Publications.

tradition or examples from ordinary day-to-day lives as a basis for faith sharing.

- Learn how to use questions to engage learners in faith sharing.

Based on the model of the catechumenate, faith sharing fosters conversion and growth in commitment to Christ. It assists learners in applying the gospel and the truths of our faith to their daily lives. Use faith sharing in some form in each of your religion sessions, whether at the beginning, as part of your prayer experience, or as part of the assimilation of the lesson.

Faith sharing that follows the readings of the liturgical seasons also helps learners be more aware of the themes of the seasons. In reflecting on these themes, the learners are living out the paschal mystery of Christ.

Step one: *lead faith sharing*

Faith sharing calls for an atmosphere of trust and respect. How do you form good relationships with your learners? What are some of the qualities you need?

- The ability to listen and to empathize.
- Patience (sometimes lots of it!) and kindness.
- The willingness to put the learners' needs above your own; knowing when to say "no."
- Sharing joys as well as sorrows.
- Recognizing their insights.
- (Pause a moment to think of any other qualities.)
- Basically, being a loving, caring person.

If you are going to be a messenger of God, sharing your faith and helping the learners share with one another, you need to show them God's love, and to trust and affirm them. No matter what age group you teach, it is important to listen to and learn about them—what they think and feel, how they express themselves. See them as individuals, not just as a group. Teach them to listen to and respect one another's contributions.

Then they will feel more comfortable sharing their own faith stories, asking questions, and discussing faith topics.

Keep the following in mind:

- Learners may refrain from sharing for various reasons, for example, family problems, poor self-image, fatigue, and so on. Getting to know the learners' interests, desires, and concerns might help draw them into the conversation. But it's also acceptable for a learner to choose not to share on a particular day.

- Advanced learners are often bored or feel that they already know all the answers. Again, it is important to know the individuals and to challenge them.

- If learners start to share information or stories that seem too personal or confidential, gently suggest that they might share that after your session, if they choose. Always make sure another adult is in the area when you meet with a child.

- If a learner begins crying during a sharing session, pause for a moment of silence and express your empathy in an appropriate way.

Step two: *share faith by presenting examples*
The first way to share faith, as the story about the American teacher in Japan illustrated, is through example.

- Share with learners (or invite them to share) stories about figures of faith in Scripture, such as Abraham, Sarah, Saint Joseph, and Mary.

- The church holds up the lives of the saints as examples of living the faith. The saints lived in various historical periods and situations. However, all had in common a great love for God and their sisters and brothers and a heroic practice of the faith.

- There are also contemporary people of faith whose example can inspire learners.

Based on the model of the catechumenate, faith sharing fosters conversion and growth in commitment to Christ.

STRATEGIES FOR TEACHING THROUGH EXAMPLES

- You can teach with examples of contemporary figures, saints from our tradition, or biblical characters in various ways, besides sharing their stories.
- Talk about who the saints are and why they are called saints.
- Use different types of activities, according to age level, to help learners apply the examples of the biblical figures and saints to their own lives. For instance, have them role play episodes from the lives of the saints that highlight the virtues of these persons.
- Help them connect the examples of the saints to passages from the gospels.
- Engage older learners in problem solving.
- Encourage them to reflect: what would St. _________ do if he or she was in this situation (one that learners might face)? How would he or she respond to the needs of the poor and oppressed and to the social injustices of today?
- With younger learners, provide means for interaction when you tell or read the stories.
- Use music related to the message of their lives.
- Show short movies or clips about the saints and discuss them.
- Assign or let the learners choose projects they can create related to the life and/or example of their favorite saints.
- Prepare prayer services or brief prayers centered on a theme from the life of the saint.
- Celebrate the feast days of the learners' saints, as well as All Saints Day.
- Remember that you and other people in the lives of learners, including the parish community, also teach by your example.

- Ask learners whom they look up to as models of Christian living and why.

Step three: *use questions to engage in faith sharing*

The example of Jesus, as well as the process of the catechumenate, offers a model for faith sharing. Jesus often asked questions, sometimes to make a point, sometimes to engage his listeners in deeper reflection, but always as a call to faith and to conversion. When he spoke about love for enemies, he asked, “For if you love those who love you, what reward do you have? Do not even the tax collectors do the same?” (Matthew 5:46). In talking about setting the right priorities in life, he asked: “Can any of you by worrying add a single hour to your span of life?” (Matthew 6:27). After Lazarus died, Jesus met Martha and told her, “Everyone who lives and believes in me will never die. Do you believe this?” (John 11:26).

In the catechumenate, persons preparing for Christian initiation engage in faith sharing as part of their journey to conversion. They apply the Sunday gospel reading to their own experiences, and each finds personal meaning in the words and actions of Jesus.

Questions leading to discussion are an effective way to begin faith sharing. Base your questions on the Sunday gospel readings, stories, current news events, and so on.

Asking questions is an often overlooked skill. We must always intentionally craft our questions in a manner appropriate to the age level toward which our question is directed. All learners need to be guided in discovering the truth for themselves. As they grow older, they will then be able to find in Scripture and church teaching the answers to the questions with which life presents them. We can begin to help even the youngest children develop this skill.

STRATEGIES FOR DIFFERENT AGE GROUPS

Faith sharing requires different approaches for different ages. Try these methods with the learners.

- Primary-age learners do not yet have the ability to think abstractly, although they are beginning to form concrete concepts. Third graders may begin to connect concrete concepts to form larger concepts. Questions need to be about specifics in the readings. For example:

Questions leading to discussion are an effective way to begin faith sharing.

What did Jesus do? What did he say? What did the prodigal son do? Was that a good thing? What did the father do? Why did the father put his arms around his son and hug him? Was that a good thing? If you were the father (or mother) would you welcome back the son? An activity suited to their age level is often a helpful way to engage them in faith sharing.

- Intermediate-age learners are more competent in connecting concrete concepts. Around the age of eleven they begin to develop the ability to think abstractly. Thus the questions you ask or help the learners ask will involve more reflection, for the most part on the concrete level. Again, activities such as simple projects, role playing, and so on can help them better grasp the message of the reading.

- Middle school learners are able to form conclusions based on abstract thinking. For them, as well as for youth, high school students, and adults, you will want to prepare good, clear, thought-provoking questions according to their age level, questions that will encourage them to share their faith. You can ask open-ended questions and questions that will lead them to make decisions, to move from ideas and beliefs to action. They also will ask questions that can help themselves and their group delve more deeply into the meaning of the Scriptures. Some means for doing this are brainstorming, small-group discussions, problem-solving, and simulations in which learners have to make decisions in real-life situations.

- Adult and young adult learners can tackle more complex, abstract questions. But it is still best to avoid "theological debate," which can sometimes replace personal sharing. (Invite the learners of all ages to put themselves into the text of Scripture.)

As you end this session

If you don't already do this, resolve to read and meditate on Scripture at least twice this week, applying its message to your daily life. Better still, do this in a group or with your family.

> Catechesis should take Sacred Scripture as its inspiration, its fundamental curriculum, and its end because it strengthens faith, nourishes the soul, and nurtures the spiritual life.
> **NDC 24B**

Catechism connection

In teaching with faith sharing, you witness to the blessing of life that is united with Christ. Read and reflect on articles 2697–2758 of the *Catechism of the Catholic Church* to explore this in greater depth.

MY THOUGHTS

SESSION

10

Using technology *in* teaching

The goal of this session is to learn when and how to make effective use of technology in your formation sessions.

YOUR OBJECTIVES ARE:

- to become familiar with the various means of communication available for catechesis
- to teach about how the media affect culture
- to learn how to organize the teaching space

SKILL: to learn strategies for making the most of technology in and outside of the session

BEGINNING THIS SESSION

Before you begin to develop your skill in using technology in teaching, take a few moments for reflection and prayer.

We don't walk alone

The name "saints" has often been used in the history of the church to address the members of the community. For example, Paul addresses his letter to the "saints who are in Ephesus" or "the saints and faithful brothers and sisters in Christ in Colossae." This seems to reinforce an understanding in the early church that sainthood and holiness were not things a person earned, but rather gifts from God bestowed on all the baptized.

We are holy because of our baptism into the body of Christ. We are brothers and sisters because we have all been marked with the sign of Christ and have become heirs of the glory of his resurrection. While we do not earn our kinship in the body of Christ, we strive to live in a way that is authentic to our identity as brothers and sisters. Not only do we receive encouragement, inspiration, and companionship from others, but we offer the same to others. We go out of our way to build up the community of Christ by offering comfort to those in sorrow, hope to those in despair, and faith to those who are struggling; by visiting those in prison; and by caring for the poor among us. This is what we do as family members in the body of Christ.

Take a moment to reflect

Ask yourself: What can I contribute to the life of the community? How can I build up the family of my church?

The time of prayer
For a few minutes, close your eyes and imagine yourself in God's presence, surrounded by loved ones and holy ones of all the ages. Let yourself stand for a while in humble reverence before the loving gaze of your God. This is the God who loves you much more than you know. All the ones around you are smiling.

God of my heart,
you know me better than I know myself,
and you understand that my
heart really wants you
to be more a part of my life.
Teach me, Lord, as you would
patiently teach a child,
how to allow you to permeate
my daily activities.
I don't think I yet comprehend
how much you love me and
want to have me close.
Thank you, Lord, from the
depths of my heart,
for those who journey with me
as brothers and sisters.

From personal reflection to sharing faith
As a catechist, you have the opportunity to share with your learners our call to live as holy people. In this session, you will develop skills in using technology in teaching in order to create an environment in which your learners may open their minds and hearts to this incredible love of God for us.

TOOLS FOR TEACHING

> The media has become essential for evangelization and catechesis. **GDC 160**

Setting the tone
Which three television programs do you watch the most? After identifying these, reflect on these questions:

Do you choose each show based on a) entertainment value, b) moral value, c) educational value, or d) other perceived value of the program? Which of these values ranked the highest as the reason for watching each program? What does this tell you about your TV viewing habits?

The importance of this session
This section presents the importance of understanding and using communication media. How can you make the means of communication an effective part of your catechesis?

- Become familiar with the various forms of technology available for catechesis.
- Teach about how the media affects culture.
- Learn strategies for making the most of the means of communication in and outside of the learning session.

Take a moment to ask yourself: Has my sense of responsibility in the use of these media grown with the same leaps and bounds as the development of the various forms of technology? Do they really contribute to the betterment of society or are some of them just the result of a consumer mentality?

Communication media can be a powerful force for good: in providing quick, accurate information, depicting values, fostering understanding and assistance among nations, sharing discoveries, and promoting education, as well as offering entertainment. But there is a dark side to communication media and their power.

As catechists, we need to learn how to use these media in our programs and to educate learners about how to use them to become better persons and followers of Christ. Media literacy is essential to help learners become discerning viewers, listeners, and users of the media. We will speak out and take action when the media promote ideas and practices and ways of life that are counter to the commandments and the teachings of Christ.

Step one: *use various means of communication*

The means of communication vary in purpose, effect, and use. Study this brief presentation of those that can be effectively employed in and outside of your learning sessions.

DVDS AND STREAMING VIDEO. Clips from popular films and TV programs can emphasize and illustrate themes of a lesson, either as an introduction or to assist assimilation. They can also be used to illustrate the influence they have on our culture and thinking.

CDS, MP3S, AND STREAMING MUSIC. Soft instrumental music can be used as background for prayer experiences. Music for young children is an excellent way to involve them in a lesson theme, especially if you use gestures or dance with it. For older children and youth, you can use some popular music to spark discussions on related themes or topics. Again, songs can be used to illustrate the influence they have on our culture and thinking.

RADIO, IPODS, TABLETS, AND CELL PHONES. While used more on an individual basis, you can discuss the use of these means, especially in connection with games and music. iPods and tablets also allow the owners to view movies as well as information.

TELEVISION. Although television programs generally cannot be used during the religion session, you can still make them part of your lesson or refer to them during a discussion. Educational programs often have information or programming that may be referred to in your lesson, for example in relation to creation, people, history, and so on. How and why do certain programs or characters become cultural icons?

COMPUTERS. One aspect of computers is their use as tools for creative activities. In addition, a world of information, formation, and fun is at your fingertips on the internet. The internet has many websites with downloadable activities. Other websites offer facts on poverty, missions, ecology, the saints, and so much more.

You can also use the computer to keep in touch with other catechists and teachers by means of email, messaging, and various social media. Online courses and degree programs are widely available, including courses from Catholic universities.

CD-ROMS, CLOUD STORAGE, AND SUBSCRIPTION SERVICES. This technology is another tool for learning, including software that provides libraries and learning paths for every age level, on a variety of subjects.

COMPUTER AND VIDEO GAMES. Varying widely in content, from educational and fun games for children to violent games for adults, video games now include more Christian games—for example, catechumenate and Bible-based games.

Each of these media has its own "language" that Catholic educators need to learn in order to present Christ's message to the people of today.

Step two: *be aware of how the media affect our culture*

For better or worse the media do affect our culture. As a catechist or teacher you need to reflect on the impact of media and share this with learners in age-appropriate ways.

In the "Decree on the Means of Social Communication," the Second Vatican Council spoke clearly about forming consciences especially with regard to three is-

Media literacy is essential to help learners become discerning viewers, listeners, and users of the media.

sues: information, the rights of art and the moral law, and the representation of good and evil.[10] Precisely in these areas the media have had a powerful impact on our culture.

It is not always easy to remember that media outlets are very particular and completely selective in choosing the information they provide, as well as the manner in which they provide it. "Reality, for many, is what the media recognize as real; what the media do not acknowledge seems of little importance."[11] For example, how do the media present the plight of the poor and marginalized? What part do they play in the consumerism and materialism of our time? How are the teachings of the church presented in the secular media? How do the media affect politics, economics, and education? How aware are we of media ownership and its increasing concentration in the hands of a small group of multinational conglomerates? If there are fewer than ten real media owners in the world, how many perspectives are really available to us as we seek to inform ourselves?

What values (or non-values) do children, youth, and adults learn from their favorite TV, film, or computer/video game characters? What challenges do they face, and how do they face them?

Step three: ***make the most of the media***

In this section, we will look at some strategies for using the media in your formation sessions and helping learners be discerning in their use of the media.

PRIMARY-AGE CHILDREN

- Ask children who their favorite TV characters are. Ask each of them to act out something their character does (a song, a phrase, a story), and to explain why they like that character.

- If you teach a lesson on forgiveness, use a video story to emphasize the theme.

- Use excerpts from a movie about friendship, and compare the types of

---

10 *Communio et Progressio*, Decree on the Means of Social Communication, nos 5–7.

11 *Aetatis Novae*, On the Twentieth Anniversary of *Communio et Progressio*, no. 4.

friendship by having the children draw pictures of the characters, or sing the songs.

- Have the children use the internet to find pages for their age level on different topics.

FOR INTERMEDIATE-AGE LEARNERS

- Ask learners to think about their favorite video or computer game (if they don't have one, they can choose a movie). Who is the hero or heroine? What challenge does he or she face? How does she or he overcome it?

- Invite learners to work in small groups. Each group should choose a popular song, draw colors to go with it, and then write down the actual words. Have each group talk about what the song says and its message. Why did they choose the color(s) they used?

- Have the children work in small groups of two or more to prepare a report about an event or happening in their school, neighborhood, or parish. After they present their reports, discuss their experience.

MIDDLE SCHOOL LEARNERS, YOUTH, HIGH SCHOOL LEARNERS, OR ADULTS

- Ask learners to keep a record of the television programs they watch over the course of a week. For at least one of the programs have them answer questions such as the following: Who are the main characters? What values do you learn from them? How would you rate this program as to its portrayal of Christian values and why? Invite them to share some of their findings.

- Arrange a panel discussion on the topic: When should the public's right to information give way to an individual's right to privacy?

- Invite learners to form small groups and role play a situation from one of the television programs or movies they have

What values (or non-values) do children, youth, and adults learn from their favorite TV, film, or computer/video game characters?

watched recently. Then ask them to role play it again, this time with a "Christian twist." What are the differences, if any?

- Ask learners to form small groups and come up with an idea for a Christian record, computer game, TV program, or whatever means they choose. Each group will then present their ideas to the larger group for feedback.

As you end this session

Reflect on how the media have influenced your life (for example, choices in clothes, political views, desire for more things, language, attitudes toward other people).

> Catechists must seriously commit themselves to learning how to use these media to bring people to Christ.
> **NDC 30**

Catechism connection

In using technology in teaching, you spread the gospel in ways your learners appreciate, as disciples have spread the Good News in their times and places throughout the centuries. Read and reflect on articles 871–945 of the *Catechism of the Catholic Church* to explore this in greater depth.

In using technology in teaching, you spread the gospel in ways your learners appreciate, as disciples have spread the Good News in their times and places throughout the centuries.

MY THOUGHTS

Final reflection

As you conclude your time of study, reflection, and sharing through this book, take a few moments in quiet reflection and prayer. Look back at your notes, the goals and objectives for each session, and all that you have learned. Then, take time to thank God for the grace of the ministry of catechesis that you offer, and ask for continued wisdom, insight, and blessing as you commit yourself to walking with your learners on the journey of discipleship.

COMPANIONS IN CHRIST

With great love, God has bestowed an abundance of grace on you as you have reflected, studied, and shared. Now, go back over the reflections you have already done in order to savor the powerful moments of grace that have been given you. You're invited to recall the graces you've been given, to relish them and find even more goodness in them.

O God, you are my God, I seek you,
My soul thirsts for you;
My flesh faints for you,
as in a dry and weary land where
there is no water. (Psalm 63)

LURED BY GOD'S LOVE

Growing in the life of the Spirit is really about falling in love. It's about a personal relationship with Jesus. It's also, of course, about doctrines, moral principles, and being able to quote Scripture, but the first step is the encounter with Christ. The fact is, the almighty and infinite God, the Creator of this vast universe, is in love with you and hopes that you will fall in love with him. At their core, these exercises are about spending time with God, allowing ourselves time to get to know him, to see him in our daily lives, and to hear him speak to us in our hearts and minds.

Nothing is more practical than finding God,
that is, than falling in love in a quite
absolute, final way.
What you are in love with, what seizes
your imagination, will affect everything.
It will decide what will get you out of bed
in the morning,
what you will do with your evenings,
how you will spend your weekends,
what you read, who you know,
what breaks your heart,

102

and what amazes you with
joy and gratitude.
Fall in love, stay in love, and it will
decide everything. **Pedro Arrupe, SJ**[12]

Have you ever seen a teenager in love? Their whole day revolves around the other person. That's all that's on their mind. They lose track of time and spend hours on the phone just talking or texting about nothing. All they desire is to be in each other's presence. As we get a little older, however, we realize that falling in love might mean that we'll have to change our way of life and reveal ourselves to the other person in unaccustomed ways, allowing the other person to experience our selfishness and sinfulness. As we lose our innocence, falling in love can sometimes take more time.

This process of falling in love is what God has been doing within you through these exercises. Through grace, God has been revealed to you and opened your heart to fuller love. God has been stretching your heart so that you can receive more love and, little by little, open up the possibility that you will fall in love with God too.

12 This quotation is attributed to Pedro Arrupe, S.J., Superior General of the Society of Jesus, 1961-1984.

There are very few people who realize what God would make of them if they abandoned themselves into his hands, and let themselves be formed by his grace.

St. Ignatius of Loyola

PILGRIM COMPANIONS

We are not alone on our journey to let God's love transform us. We have many other travelers to stand with, men and women who have the same dreams, experience the same struggles, and hold on to the same hopeful promise. When we are discouraged, the faith of those other travelers can raise us up and give us the strength and desire to continue. God provides such pilgrims as a gift to us. They are men and women who desire, as we do, to know God more intimately, and so to fall in love with him.

The time of prayer

Close your eyes and imagine God's face before you. God is proud of and takes great delight in you. End with the following prayer, or better, with a prayer in your own words.

Dear God, Lord of Love,
I sit here feeling nervous before
the gaze of your love.
I'm not accustomed to letting you
look at me in this way.
The power and depth of your love
take my breath away.
Forgive me if I'm not yet able to give
myself to you completely,
not yet able to fall in love with you.
I can't even fathom what
that would feel like.
Make up for what is lacking
in my desire, Lord.
Let the fire of your love transform me
so that I can become a better disciple,
a better teacher and bearer of your word.

[OF RELATED INTEREST]

Our Catholic Life

A READING AND STUDY GUIDE FOR ADULT FAITH FORMATION

A program based on the four parts of THE CATECHISM OF THE CATHOLIC CHURCH

CREED + SACRAMENTS + COMMANDMENTS + PRAYER

Written for Today's Catholics:

- A dynamic pedagogy for use in small groups (RCIA, catechist formation, catechists, adult study groups)
- Discussion questions leading to critical conversations about faith in the contemporary world
- Affordably priced
- Imprimatur
- Available in English and Spanish editions
- A FREE, comprehensive Leader's Guide is available on our website.

Bulk pricing

1-19 COPIES	$6.95 EACH
20-49 COPIES	$5.95 EACH
50-99 COPIES	$4.95 EACH
100 + COPIES	$3.95 EACH

BOOKS IN THE SERIES

The Human Journey of Faith (Creed)
Main themes:
- The Inborn Hunger for God
- The Response to Revelation is Faith
- Made in God's Image

The Mystery of God (Creed)
Main themes:
- God Reveals his Loving Plan of Goodness
- Sacred Scripture is the Word of God
- I Believe in God the Father

Drawing Closer to Christ (Creed)
Main themes:
- Jesus Christ: The Only Son of God
- Mary: Mother of God and Mother of the Church
- The Reign of God

The Mystery of the Church (Creed)
Main Themes:
- The Church hands on Divine Revelation
- The Mystery of the Church
- One, Holy, Catholic, Apostolic

Living the Sacraments (Sacraments)
Main themes:
- Baptism
- Confirmation
- Eucharist

Living the Commandments (Commandments)
Main themes:
- No Strange gods
- Keeping Holy the Lord's Day
- Honoring our Parents

Praying our Way through Life (Prayer)
Main themes:
- The Liturgy is the Work of the Trinity
- The People, Places, and Rites of the Liturgy
- Called to an Encounter with God

All books available in Spainsh

A **FREE**, COMPREHENSIVE LEADER'S GUIDE IS AVAILABLE ON OUR WEBSITE.

TO ORDER CALL 1-800-321-0411
OR VISIT WWW.TWENTYTHIRDPUBLICATIONS.COM

TWENTY-THIRD PUBLICATIONS
A division of Bayard, Inc.